home knits

LUXURIOUS HANDKNITS FOR EVERY ROOM OF THE HOUSE

home
knits

LUXURIOUS HANDKNITS

FOR EVERY ROOM

OF THE HOUSE

SUSS COUSINS

photographs by
MICHAEL WESCHLER

A Lark Production

POTTER
CRAFT

New York

Copyright © 2006 by Suss Cousins
Photographs copyright © by Michael Weschler

Published in the United States by Potter Craft, an imprint
of the Crown Publishing Group, a division of Random
House, Inc., New York.
www.crownpublishing.com
www.clarksonpotter.com

POTTER CRAFT and CLARKSON N. POTTER are
trademarks, and POTTER and colophon are registered
trademarks of Random House, Inc.

Library of Congress Cataloging-in-Publication Data is
available upon request

ISBN-10: 0-307-33591-7
ISBN-13: 978-0-307-33591-3

Printed in China

Design by Jan Derevjanik
Photography by Michael Weschler

10 9 8 7 6 5 4 3 2 1

First Edition

contents

Introduction.......6

LIVING ROOM

Lively Striped Lampshade.......14

Leaf Lampshade.......18

Buttoned-Up Curtain Tieback.......24

Big Pillow Cover.......28

Basketweave Pillow.......32

Jute Coasters.......36

Knitted Art.......38

Ottoman Cozy.......42

Art Wall Hanging.......46

Pastel Patchwork Throw.......50

DINING ROOM AND KITCHEN

Striped Seat Covers.......58

Beaded Placemats.......62

Chair Covers with Ribbon Ties.......66

Napkin Holder with Button.......70

Crystal Table Runner.......74

Knitted Guestbook.......78

Two-Tone Kitchen Curtains.......82

Tote Bag.......86

Basketweave Rug.......90

Embroidered Vase Cover.......94

BEDROOM AND BATH

Alpaca Lampshades.......102

Swedish Bed Canopy.......106

Fantasy Pillows.......110

Multi–Yarn Shawl.......114

Ultrasuede Hanger Cover.......118

Kimono Robe.......122

Luxurious Bedcover.......130

Monogrammed Guest Towels.......134

Eyeglass Case with Button Closure.......138

Drawstring Shoe Bag.......142

Yarn Substitution Guide.......146

Index of Projects and Yarns.......148

Resources.......154

About the Author.......157

Acknowledgments.......158

Index.......160

introduction

Welcome to Suss Cousins's *Home Knits*! I've been imagining this book for a long time, and I'm happy to be sharing my vision of the comforts of home and knitting with you.

It all started one evening two years ago, when my husband and I were sitting in our living room. We were having some wine while appreciating a painting we had just bought. Called *The Woman,* it shows a figure surrounded by a geometric pattern of green, turquoise, chocolate, and orange. The longer I looked at it, the more I realized it just didn't fit the style of our house. Or rather, our house somehow did not welcome the painting. So I said, "Let's move!" We move every few years and I get to decorate all over again, which I love to do.

We found the perfect house for our painting, and it, together with a trip back to Sweden, inspired a new direction of decor. I wanted a soothing, calm feeling, now that I'm a bit older and I work such long, intense hours. Our old house was sort of Spanish Gothic, with lots of arched doorways and curves, whereas the new house is quite simple and more modern, with straight lines. I used earthy, neutral colors with accents of bright green, orange, turquoise, and red. Our furniture is more geometric, too, like the painting. It reminds me a lot of Swedish homes and the house I grew up in during the 1960s.

Back then, the usual decor was all fuzzy rugs, leather couches, blond wood, and plenty of white with very bright colors. My room was chocolate and cream, with little red accents and a leopard-pattern throw on my bed. My mother is an artist, and she loved to repaint the kitchen every year or so. Sometimes it would be yellow, other times orange. One time she stenciled hearts on the door. She rearranged the furniture constantly, painting the chairs. It was another aspect of her creativity, and I got all my love of decorating—and change!—from her.

When she found out we had moved to a new house, she sent me a dozen small, square black and gold paintings, which are perfect. Once I knew we were moving, I couldn't stop thinking of home knits for our new house. From lampshades to wall hangings, from kitchen curtains to curtain tiebacks, I imagined new patterns every day. So gradually over the last year, I knit every item you see in these pages—all the photographs were taken in my own home. This book, like my home, is about classic, timeless texture and color, distinctive and vivid. Because I was using a more subdued color palette, I wanted to emphasize texture. I used nubby, tweedy wool, pebbly leather and suede, soft, fuzzy yarn, thick string, strips of fabric, bamboo, and wood to create a sensory explosion.

I also like to mix old stuff with the new. That's the way I decorated our house, which I did in one week while the rest of my family was out of town. It was a little crazy and a lot of fun. I began by hanging *The Woman* in the living room and added a waterfall of strands of sparkly yarn, an old wooden armoire, cream-colored velvet chairs, and bright square pillows in leather and yarn. An antique mirror and handblown Swedish glass went over the fireplace.

The dining room evolved from a 1950s art deco table-and-leather-chairs set that I could never part with.

I found a huge fan with a lamp to hang above the table and added thick rustic wooden shutters. My kitchen is all white with stainless-steel appliances, natural-colored tile, a brown leather rug in front of the sink, heavy silver cabinet knobs, and orchids everywhere.

In our backyard, I hung a large candelabrum and put handknit pillows on wrought-iron chairs arranged around a big rough wooden table. The landscaping is just rock and grass. I did it all with almost no money. You don't need a lot of money to make a space beautiful. I buy things like twine, colored glass, and small stones; that's how I decorate. I often pick up items at home improvement stores to transform into still lives in my store or my home. For example, I'll take a huge earthenware pot with a nice patina, fill it with an arrangement of bamboo, and place it in a corner. I save my big splurges for flowers. I always, *always* have fresh flowers all over the house. Lucky for me, friends and family have made me gifts of many beautiful vases, knowing how important flowers are to me.

I think the best decorating is simple. If you surround yourself only with objects, colors, art, and materials that you love, you can't go wrong. I've tried to fill this book with items you will love to knit and then love to live with. The projects range from easy ones you can complete in a few hours—napkin rings, a shoe bag— to more complex items that will take more time but will return your investment for years—such as a bed canopy or luxurious bathrobes for the whole family.

I hope the projects in this book make you happy to come home . . . and even happier to stay home and knit!

living room

lively striped lampshade

After traveling to three different stores and not
finding a cute lampshade for my living room,
I decided to knit my own.

lively striped lampshade {intermediate}

Be careful to pick the right color of yarn and knit loosely enough for the light to shine through your fabric. The rich chocolate brown striped with cream has a very clean, modern, Scandinavian look to it.

SIZE

One size to fit drum lampshade measuring 13"/33 cm in diameter × 14"/35.5 cm high

FINISHED MEASUREMENTS

18"/45.5 cm wide × 43"/109 cm long (before seaming)

YARN

A: 2 skeins Suss Cotton (100% cotton; 2.5 ounces/71 grams; 118 yards/109 meters), color crocodile

B: 4 skeins Suss Cotton (100% cotton; 2.5 ounces/71 grams; 118 yards/109 meters), color natural

NOTIONS

1 pair size 10 (6mm) needles

20 sewing pins

1 sewing needle and thread, color cream

1 tapestry needle

2 large safety pins

1 drum lampshade 13"/33 cm in diameter × 14"/35.5 cm high

Small safety pins (optional)

GAUGE

16 stitches and 20 rows = 4"/10 cm in stockinette stitch

making the lampshade

Cast on 72 stitches with yarn A.

Work in stockinette stitch (knit right-side rows, purl wrong-side rows) for 6 rows, beginning with a right-side row.

Work 18 rows in yarn B.

Work 12 rows in yarn A.

Work 24 rows in yarn B.

Work 8 rows in yarn A.

Work 24 rows in yarn B.

Work 12 rows in yarn A.

Work 18 rows in yarn B.

Work 6 rows in yarn A.

Work 24 rows in yarn B.

Work 18 rows in yarn A.

Work 12 rows in yarn B.

Work 6 rows in yarn A.

Work 28 rows in yarn B.

You should have 216 rows total. Bind off.

finishing

Weave in all loose ends with the tapestry needle.

Fold each long edge over 1"/2.5 cm towards wrong side, and pin down with sewing pins. Whipstitch this seam using the sewing needle and cream-colored thread, making sure that stitches are not visible on right side. Make sure the top and bottom seams are wide enough to allow you to thread the elastic through the channels.

Turn the piece over so the right side is facing outward and fold so that the short (cast-on and bind-off) edges meet. Use an invisible join (described below), or whipstitch the two edges together, working between the seamed channel you have sewn down the long sides of the fabric. Leave the inside, or wrong side, of these channels open for the time being, as you will need these openings to thread elastic through the top and bottom of the finished lampshade. You may want to use safety pins to hold the edges together while you join them.

INVISIBLE JOIN: Place the two short edges side by side, with the top of the cast-on edge meeting the bottom of the bind-off edge, to form a tube. Line up the stitches. Working from left to right, find the first stitch that follows the seamed channel sewn down the long edge of the fabric. Using a large tapestry needle and yarn B, insert the needle into that first stitch of the cast-on edge as if you were going to purl (purlwise). Then insert the needle into the corresponding first stitch on the bind-off edge (that is, the first stitch after the seamed channel) as if you were going to knit (knitwise). You have now completed the establishing stitch.

Repeat as follows: Insert the needle knitwise into the same first stitch on the cast-on edge, and then insert the needle purlwise into the *second* stitch on the cast-on edge. Next, insert the needle purlwise into the first stitch on the bind-off edge, and then insert the needle knitwise into the second stitch on the bind-off edge. Repeat this process until you reach the final stitch before the seamed channel on the other long side, pulling the yarn tight every few stitches. The joining seam should be nearly invisible. With the tapestry needle, weave in any loose ends.

Cut the elastic in half. Attach the end of one half to one of the large safety pins. Thread the safety pin through the top channel, taking care to hold on to the other end of the elastic. Pin the two ends of the elastic together. Repeat this process on the bottom channel.

Test the size of the finished piece by fitting it over the lampshade. The cover should fit snugly over the lampshade but should also be loose enough that you can take it on and off for cleaning. The elastic should be tight enough to hold the piece in place. For the top channel, remove the safety pin and tie the two ends of the elastic together to give the piece the desired circumference. Repeat for the bottom channel. Take the piece off the lampshade and stitch up the top and bottom channel openings.

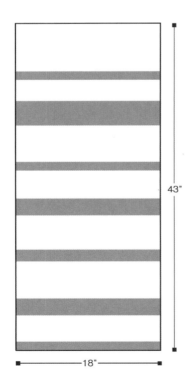

43"

18"

leaf lampshade

I designed this intarsia lampshade using a real leaf from an elm tree, and then I couldn't stop. I knit lampshades with orchids, tree branches, lilies, and willows. I love bringing the beauty of the natural world into my home.

leaf lampshade {intermediate}

The embroidery around the leaf adds even more texture and interest to the contrast between the soft knit and the hard ceramic lamp base of ivory striped with brown. You can get very different effects by using different lamp bases—from Swedish modern, as I've done here, to Japanese using a black-lacquered wood base. For a more classic home, try a gold-toned base. After you've made the lampshade, you could make the same design on a pillow and a throw.

SIZE

One size, to fit drum lampshade measuring 20"/51 cm in diameter × 12"/30 cm high

FINISHED MEASUREMENTS

Each panel measures 32"/81 cm × 22"/56.5 cm (before seaming)

YARN

A: 7 skeins Suss Mohair (76.5% mohair/17.5% wool/6% nylon; 1.5 ounces/43 grams; 102 yards/94 meters), color natural

B: 1 skein Suss Mohair (76.5% mohair/17.5% wool/6% nylon; 1.5 ounces/43 grams; 102 yards/94 meters), color jade green

C: 1 skein Suss Cotton (100% cotton; 2.5 ounces/71 grams; 118 yards/109 meters), color honey

NOTIONS

1 pair size 9 (5.5 mm) circular needles, 24"/61 cm long

Knitting row counter (recommended)

1 sewing needle and thread, color cream

Large tapestry needle

2 large safety pins

3.5 yards/3.2 meters beading cord elastic

1 drum lampshade (20"/51 cm in diameter × 12"/30 cm high), color solid white or cream

Several straight pins or safety pins (optional)

Yarn bobbins for intarsia (optional)

GAUGE

15 stitches and 20 rows = 4"/10 cm in stockinette stitch

making the lampshade

This piece is knit in two panels.

panel one

Cast on 120 stitches with yarn A.

Work in stockinette stitch (knit right-side rows, purl wrong-side rows) for 30 rows, beginning with a right-side row.

Beginning with row 31, knit 81 stitches and start working the leaf pattern with yarn B using the intarsia technique (see chart for Panel One, begin with stitch 39 of chart).

To work intarsia, use a separate ball of yarn for each color section and, when you change colors, twist the strands of each color around each other to prevent holes. You may find it helpful to put each color yarn on a separate yarn bobbin.

After you have completed all 49 rows of the leaf pattern, continue working in yarn A in stockinette stitch for 30 rows (109 rows total). Bind off loosely.

panel two

Cast on 120 stitches with yarn A. Work in stockinette stitch for 30 rows, beginning with right-side row. Beginning on row 31, knit 36 stitches and start working the leaf pattern with yarn B using the intarsia technique (see chart for Panel Two, begin with stitch 1 of chart). The Panel Two chart is a mirror image of the chart for Panel One.

After you have completed all 49 rows of the leaf pattern, continue working in yarn A in stockinette stitch for 30 rows (109 rows total). Bind off loosely.

finishing

Weave in all loose ends with the tapestry needle.

Thread tapestry needle with yarn C and make a small knot at end. Insert the needle (from the back to the front) into Panel One at the bottom of the leaf stem. Embroider in chain stitch all the way around the outline of the leaf. Knot the ends together at the back of the work and cut off the excess yarn. Keep your beginning and end knots very small so they don't show through the delicate mohair knit when the lamp is lit.
Thread the tapestry needle with another length of yarn C. Beginning in center of leaf, work a line of chain stitch with three perpendicular curved lines through the first line (as illustrated in pattern diagrams).

Work the same embroidery outline on Panel Two.

Place the two panels side by side, with short edges together and the right sides facing you. Thread the tapestry needle with yarn A. Sew together the short edges using whipstitch or an invisible vertical join.

INVISIBLE VERTICAL JOIN: Arrange the two panels with short edges together so that the rows are aligned. You may find it helpful to pin the pieces together with straight pins or safety pins as you work. Starting at the bottom of the panel on your left, insert the tapestry needle under the horizontal bar between the first and second stitches. Then insert the needle under the corresponding horizontal bar on the piece to your right. Draw the pieces together so the two stitch halves resemble one complete knit stitch. Continue alternating from the piece on your left to the right all the way up the seam. Make a knot and use the tapestry needle to weave in the loose ends.

Sew the other seam the same way to create a tube shape.

Fold over the top $1^1/2$"/3.8 cm of the tube inward, with wrong sides together. Using the sewing needle and thread, whipstitch the edge to create a channel for the elastic. Take care that the stitches look neat on the right side of the piece. Leave a small opening at the seam to insert the elastic.

Repeat the process at the bottom edge of the tube.

Cut a piece of elastic approximately 60"/152 cm. Attach a safety pin to one end of the elastic and thread through the top channel, holding on to the other end of the elastic. Pin the ends of the elastic together.

Repeat the process to thread elastic through bottom channel.

Test size of piece by fitting over the lampshade. The elasticized channels should fit snugly *inside* the top and bottom rims of the lampshade, yet piece should be loose enough to allow the lampshade to be taken on and off easily. Tie elastic to desired length. Remove piece from lampshade and cut off any excess elastic. Sew up the small channel openings.

Stretch the lampshade cover over the drum lampshade and adjust it so it lies smoothly and the stitches line up vertically. Attach your new lampshade to your lamp, turn on the light, and watch it glow.

panel one

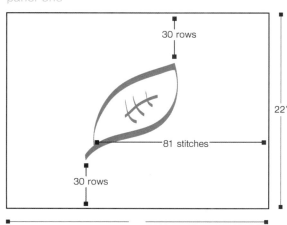

panel two

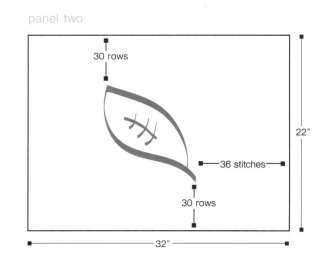

panel one

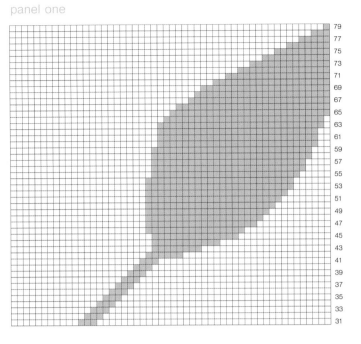

79
77
75
73
71
69
67
65
63
61
59
57
55
53
51
49
47
45
43
41
39
37
35
33
31

panel two

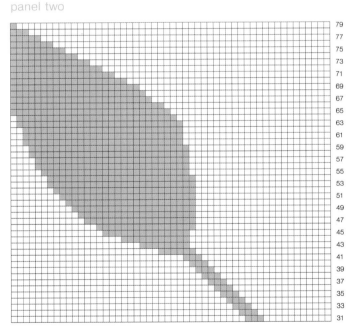

79
77
75
73
71
69
67
65
63
61
59
57
55
53
51
49
47
45
43
41
39
37
35
33
31

buttoned-up curtain tieback

I was inspired to make these tiebacks when I hung a heavy
velvet curtain to divide my living and dining rooms. I didn't
want a door to separate the room, but, rather, a softly
draped curtain I could close easily.

buttoned–up curtain tieback

Knit with cream-colored cotton tape in a simple rib pattern, the tieback is a perfect way to complement the velvet brown. I used the biggest mother-of-pearl button I could find to make it more decorative, and I don't have to worry about tying a bow! (A wooden button here would look too plain.) You can substitute an antique pin as long as you find one that's suitably large and sparkly. Try knitting this project in any chunky yarn with huge needles—it's the texture that makes it so appealing.

FINISHED MEASUREMENTS

5"/12.5 cm wide × 16"/40.5 cm long (not including button loop)

YARN

2 skeins 1"/2.5 cm wide cotton twill tape (100% cotton twill tape; 4 ounces/114 grams; 32 yards/30 meters), color natural

NOTIONS

1 pair size 19 (15 mm) needles

Large tapestry needle

1 size P (10 mm) crochet hook

Darning needle and sewing thread, color off-white

1 round mother-of-pearl button, $1^{1}/_{2}$"/4.5 cm in diameter

GAUGE

5.5 stitches and 7 rows = 4"/10 cm in rib stitch

making the buttoned–up curtain tieback

With two strands of cotton twill tape, cast on 7 stitches.

Work in one-by-one rib stitch for 28 rows, approximately 16"/40.5 cm.

Row 1: Knit 1, purl 1, repeat until the end of the row.

Row 2: Purl 1, knit 1, repeat until the end of the row. Repeat rows 1 and 2. Bind off loosely and weave in any loose ends with the tapestry needle.

Using two strands of cotton twill tape, work a single crochet around all four edges of the tieback, starting in the center of one of the narrow edges. When you've worked around all the edges back to your starting point, crochet a loop of 10 chain stitches. Attach this loop to the tieback with a single crochet stitch, and bind off tightly.

With the darning needle and sewing thread, attach the mother-of-pearl button approximately 1"/2.5 cm from the middle of the edge opposite the loop closure. The button's edge should be even with the crochet edging of the tieback. Fold the tieback around a curtain and button it closed.

buttonhole
loop

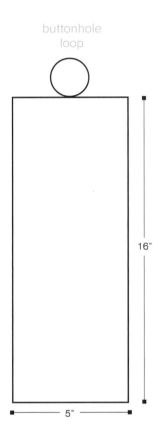

16"

5"

big pillow cover

I believe you can never have too many
pillows. From tiny cushions to elegant
bolsters, I love them all. But I think this
big, striped pillow cover is one of the
most useful things you can knit.

big pillow cover {easy}

A couple of years ago we went to a Moroccan restaurant for a friend's birthday party. The setting was beautiful, and we sat on the floor, which was covered with orange beaded pillows. I was inspired to make these big cushy pillows in greens and oranges with wood beaded tassels. The mix of yarns creates a great textured look. You can pile pillows up in decorative towers when you aren't using them and spread them around when your knitting girlfriends are coming over.

SIZE
One size to fit pillow measuring 24"/61 cm × 24"/61 cm

FINISHED MEASUREMENTS
Each panel measures 24"/61 cm × 24"/61 cm

YARN
A: 3 skeins Suss Coolaid (85% acrylic/15% wool; 2 ounces/ 57 grams; 90 yards/83 meters), color moss

B: 5 skeins Suss Candy (40% mohair/30% rayon/30% polyester; 1.5 ounces/43 grams; 47 yards/43 meters), color green moss

C: 6 skeins Suss Feather (100% polyamide; 2.5 ounces/57 grams; 145 yards/135 meters), color honey

D: 6 skeins Suss Coolaid (85% acrylic/15% wool; 2 ounces/ 57 grams; 90 yards/83 meters), color honey

E: 3 skeins Suss Fuzzy (60% cotton/40% polyamide; 2 ounces/57 grams; 67 yards/62 meters), color cantaloupe with brick red

NOTIONS
1 pair size 9 (5.5 mm) needles
1 large floor pillow (24"/61 cm × 24" /61 cm), color white or cream
Large tapestry needle
Several safety pins (optional)
1 size I (5.5 mm) crochet hook
Several large wooden beads

GAUGE
16 stitches and 20 rows = 4"/10 cm in stockinette stitch

making the pillow cover

front panel

Cast on 96 stitches with yarn A.

Begin stripe pattern: Work 4 rows in stockinette stitch (knit right-side rows, purl wrong-side rows), beginning with a right-side row.

Change to yarn B and work 24 rows of stockinette stitch.

Change to a double strand consisting of one strand yarn C and one strand of yarn D and work in stockinette stitch for 10 rows.

Change to yarn E and work in stockinette stitch for 24 rows. Repeat this pattern until the front cover measures 24"/61 cm in length, or approximately 120 rows. Bind off.

back panel

With one strand of yarn C and one strand of yarn D, cast on 96 stitches.

Work in stockinette stitch until the back cover measures 24"/61 centimeters in length, or approximately 120 rows. Make sure that the length of the back cover matches the front.

Bind off loosely.

finishing

Weave in all loose ends with the tapestry needle.

Place the two panels with the right sides facing each other. With the tapestry needle and yarn D, whipstitch three of the edges together. You might find it helpful to pin the pillow together with safety pins before you begin seaming. Leave one seam open to insert the pillow into the cover.

Place the pillow inside the knitted pillow cover. With the tapestry needle and yarn E, whipstitch the final seam closed.

With the crochet hook and yarn A, attach a chain stitch loop about 2"/5 cm long to one of the corners of the pillow. Each end of the loop should be attached securely with a single crochet stitch about 3/4"/2 cm from the corner. Repeat for the other three corners of the pillow.

tassels

Cut yarn A into 40 lengths of 16"/40.5 cm each. Fold 10 pieces in half, making a loop. Insert the loop through one of the crochet chains at the corners of the pillow. Thread the ends of the pieces through the loop you made with the fold and pull it tight. Repeat for the other three corners.

Attach about four beads—or as many as you want—to the fringe of each of the tassels by threading the bead through one piece of yarn and using another piece to tie a small knot right below the bead.

front pillow cover

FOLLOW STRIPE PATTERN

24"

24"

back pillow cover

24"

24"

basketweave pillow

One day, while looking at the basket I keep on my desk for my sketching pens and pencils, I came up with the idea to make a pillow that looks like a basket. I decided to knit strips of cotton and then weave them with strips of leather for lots of added texture.

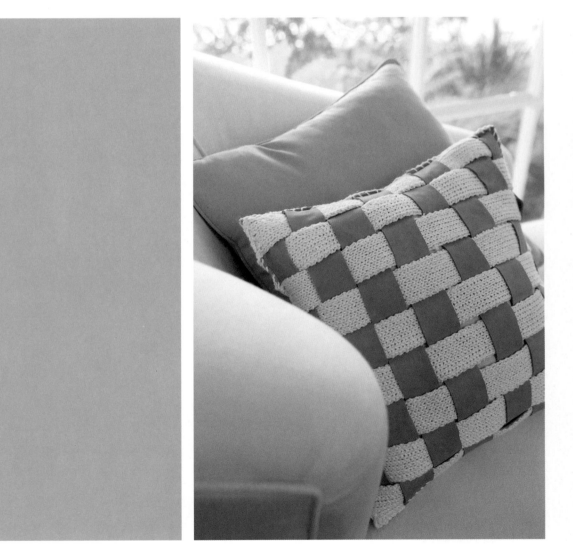

basketweave pillow {intermediate}

In this pattern, you make just one piece to sew to the top of an inexpensive cotton pillow. It looks complicated but is actually very simple once you arrange your strips. You can vary the pattern by using yarn and linen, yarn and yarn, yarn and felt—so many possibilities! Knit in one-by-one rib for a fabric that doesn't curl in at the edges, the pillow is a great gift. Make it in neutral colors to go with anyone's decor.

SIZE

One size to fit pillow measuring 18"/45.5 cm × 18"/45.5 cm

FINISHED MEASUREMENT

Each strip measures $1^3/_4$"/4.5 cm wide × 18"/45.5 cm long

YARN

4 skeins Suss Cotton (100% cotton; 2.5 ounces/71 grams; 118 yards/109 meters) color natural

NOTIONS

1 pair size 6 (4 mm) needles

1 piece of leather or Ultrasuede 20" × 20"

Leather hole puncher

Tapestry needle

1 18" × 18" pillow with off-white cotton or Ultrasuede cover

40 sewing pins

GAUGE

32 stitches and 20 rows = 4" in rib stitch

making the basketweave pillow

Cast on 14 stitches.

Work in one-by-one rib (knit 1 stitch, purl 1 stitch; repeat until the end of the row) for 18"/45.5 cm, or approximately 90 rows. Bind off.

Repeat nine times for 10 pieces total (see diagram).

finishing

Weave in all loose ends with tapestry needle. Cut the leather (or ultrasuede) into 10 strips each measuring $1^3/_4$"/4.5 cm × 18"/45.5 cm.

With the leather punch, make holes for sewing the leather to pillow. On 8 strips of leather make 4 evenly spaced holes on each short edge (see diagram 2). On the remaining 2 strips make 40 evenly spaced holes along the long edge and 3 along the short edges (see diagram 3).

To assemble, arrange all 10 knitted strips face-up next to each other. Weave one of the leather strips with the 40 holes under the first strip of knit on the far left and over the strip to its right, continuing to weave under and over all 10 knitted strips (see diagram 4). Using one pin per strip, pin the leather strip in place using some of the 40 holes. Now take one of the leather strips with 8 holes and, beginning on the far left again, start to weave it through the knitted pieces. You should see a basketweave pattern starting to develop. Continue weaving the remainder of the leather strips with the knitted strips. Reserve for last the second leather strip with 40 holes. Pull the rows close together. To hold the pieces in place, pin the leather strips and the knitted pieces together through the holes you punched. Lift up the basketweave assembly and place it on top of an 18"/45.5 cm × 18"/45.5 cm pillow. You'll notice that the basketweave top is made a little smaller than the pillow to ensure a snug fit. The top will stretch a little and fit perfectly. Thread the tapestry needle with yarn and whipstitch the basketweave assembly to the seam of the pillow all the way around and through the holes in the leather. Remove all the pins.

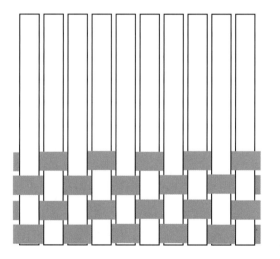

jute coasters

Experiment with knitting these coasters in different yarns and needles if you want a softer look. Cream-colored cotton, for example, would look very nice in a room with light walls and wood.

jute coasters {beginner}

Jute twine knits up into such an interesting, earthy texture that I had to include it somewhere in this book. These cute coasters are the easiest project ever, not to mention fast and inexpensive. They're also very durable. When my husband and his friends put their drinks down on these coasters, I don't worry—they can stand up to anything. A set of coasters would make a great gift. Cut a piece of twine 40 inches long and tie it around a stack of four coasters the next time you need a special gift in a hurry.

FINISHED MEASUREMENTS

4¹/₄"/11 cm × 4¹/₄"/11 cm

YARN

1 roll natural jute twine (3-ply medium weight, 208 feet/64 meters) (available at most hardware stores)

NOTIONS

1 pair size 9 (5.5 mm) needles

Tapestry needle

GAUGE

10 stitches and 14 rows = 4"/10cm in seed stitch

making the coasters

Cast on 11 stitches loosely.

Row 1: Knit 1, purl 1, and repeat this pattern until the end of the row.

Row 2: Knit the purl stitches and purl the knit stitches across the row.

Repeat until piece measures 4¹/₄"/11 cm, approximately 15 rows.

Bind off stitches loosely following the seed stitch pattern.

Make three more coasters for a total of four.

finishing

Weave in all loose ends with the tapestry needle.

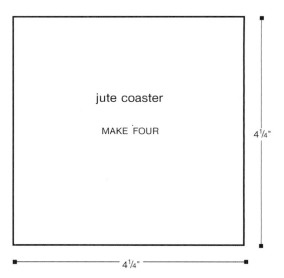

jute coaster

MAKE FOUR

4¹/₄"

4¹/₄"

knitted art

My daughter Hanna is an artist who paints in oils. But I believe we are all artists! So when she did a painting with red, orange, yellow, and green circles, I translated it into this wall hanging. I think this color combination has a great look, but of course you can use any colors that you love!

knitted art {experienced}

To create the wall hanging, I knit a small rectangle in chocolate yarn with colored dots. The front panel is knit using the intarsia technique; the four small side panels cover the canvas. Staple the finished piece to the canvas before hanging.

SIZE

One size to fit a canvas 14"/35.5 cm wide × 11"/28 cm long

FINISHED MEASUREMENTS

Front Panel: 14"/35.5 cm wide × 11"/28 cm long

Top and Bottom Panels: 14"/35.5 cm wide × 2¹/₂"/6.5 cm long

Side Panels: 11"/35.5 cm wide × 2¹/₂"/6.5 cm long

YARN

A: 3 skeins Suss Twisted (100% cotton; 2.5 ounces/71 grams; 108 yards/98 meters), color chocolate

B: 1 skein Suss Mohair (76.5% mohair/17.5% wool/6% nylon; 1.5 ounces/43 grams; 102 yards/94 meters), color pebble

C: 1 skein Suss Mohair (76.5% mohair/17.5% wool/6% nylon; 1.5 ounces/43 grams; 102 yards/94 meters), color winged teal

NOTIONS

1 pair size 7 (4.5 mm) needles

Yarn bobbins for intarsia (optional)

Tapestry needle

1 painting canvas 11"/28 cm × 14"/35.5 cm

Staple gun and staples (available at any hardware store)

4 small hooks, ¹/₂" diameter

1 ball twine or other rope

GAUGE

16 stitches and 27 rows = 4"/10 cm in stockinette stitch

For this piece, it is very important to check gauge.

making the knitted art piece

front panel

Cast on 58 stitches with yarn A. Work in stockinette stitch (knit right-side rows and purl wrong-side rows) for 14 rows, beginning with a right-side row.

At row 15, knit 15 stitches and then begin the intarsia pattern (see chart). To work intarsia, use a separate ball of yarn for each color section. When you change colors twist the strands of each color around each other to prevent holes. You might find it helpful to put each color yarn on a separate yarn bobbin. With yarn B, knit 2 stitches. Change to yarn A and knit 24 stitches. Begin the second intarsia circle with yarn C, knit 2 stitches. Knit the last 15 stitches with yarn A. Continue following the intarsia pattern for a total of 14 rows.

Knit 18 rows in stockinette with yarn A.

On row 47, begin following the intarsia pattern as you did for the first pair of circles. However, with this pair of circles, you will begin with yarn C, followed by yarn B (see chart).

Knit in stockinette stitch with yarn A for another 14 rows (74 rows total). Bind off.

top and bottom panels
Cast on 58 stitches with yarn A. Beginning with a right-side row, work in stockinette stitch for 2$\frac{1}{2}$"/6.5 cm, or approximately 18 rows. Bind off.

Repeat and make a second panel.

side panels
Cast on 44 stitches with yarn A. Beginning with a right-side row, work in stockinette stitch for 2$\frac{1}{2}$"/6.5 cm, or approximately 18 rows. Bind off.

Repeat and make a second side panel.

finishing
Weave in all loose ends with the tapestry needle.

With yarn A, sew the top and bottom panels to the top and bottom edges of the front panel. Make sure to line up the stitches so the pieces lie evenly. Sew the side panels to the side edges of the front panel in a similar fashion, making sure that all the stitches and rows lie straight. Whipstitch the short edges of the side pieces to the short edges of the top and bottom pieces.

Stretch the knitted cover over the front of the canvas and then place it front-side down. Fold over the sides of the knitted cover, lay the corners flat and, using the staple gun, staple the corners of the cover to the wooden frame on the back of the canvas. Continue stapling the rest of the cover to the back. As you staple the rest of the piece, make sure that the stitches and rows are lined up evenly and that the knitted front lies flat on the canvas.

Screw hooks into the top of the covered canvas approximately 2"/5 cm from the sides, and 10"/25.5 cm apart from each other. Screw two corresponding hooks into your ceiling 10"/25.5 cm apart and approximately 5"/12.5 cm from the wall. With twine, yarn, or some other kind of rope that matches your décor, tie the hooks in the wall hanging to the hooks in the ceiling.

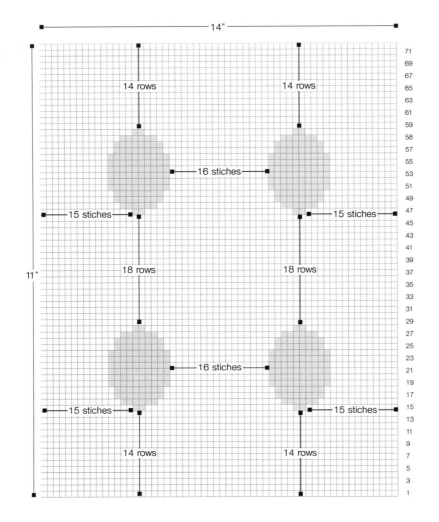

14"

71
69
67
65
63
61
59
58
57
55
53
51
49
47
45
43
41
39
37
35
33
31
29
27
25
23
21
19
17
15
13
11
9
7
5
3
1

14 rows   14 rows

16 stiches

15 stiches   15 stiches

11"   18 rows   18 rows

16 stiches

15 stiches   15 stiches

14 rows   14 rows

MAKE TWO

14"

MAKE TWO

2½"

11"

ottoman cozy

An ottoman is one of the most essential pieces of furniture you can own. It's so versatile! You can move it around to wherever it's most needed, use it as a footrest or for extra seating, then tuck it out of the way. I like to place my hand-painted wooden tray on top to serve as an instant coffee table.

ottoman cozy {intermediate}

Covering an old ottoman in this beautifully variegated yarn can freshen up your living area. The finishing crochet stitch gives it a handcrafted look and makes it extra durable. It's lucky that the pattern is very easy because I think you'll want more than one.

SIZE

One size to fit an ottoman measuring 20"/51 cm × 20"/51 cm × 14"/35.5 cm

FINISHED MEASUREMENTS

Each square is 19"/48 cm × 19"/48 cm

Each rectangle is 19"/48 cm × 14"/35.5 cm

YARN

12 skeins Suss Handpainted (100% wool; 3.5 oz/100 g; 56 yards/52 meters), color grassroots

NOTIONS

1 pair size 11 (8 mm) needles

Tapestry needle

Safety pins or sewing pins

1 size I (5.5 mm) crochet hook

1 ottoman measuring approximately 20"/51 cm × 20"/51 cm × 14"/35.5 cm

GAUGE

12 stitches and 16 rows = 4"/10 cm in stockinette stitch

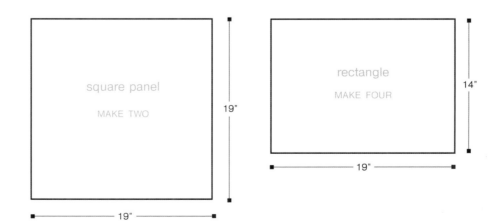

square panel
MAKE TWO

19"

19"

rectangle
MAKE FOUR

14"

19"

making the ottoman cozy

You make two square panels and four smaller rectangular panels to cover the ottoman. The two square panels cover the top and bottom of the ottoman, and the smaller rectangular panels cover the sides.

square panel

Cast on 56 stitches.

Work in stockinette stitch (knit right-side rows and purl wrong-side row) for 19"/48 cm (or approximately 76 rows), beginning with a right-side row. Bind off.

Make two square panels.

rectangular panel

Cast on 56 stitches.

Work in stockinette stitch for 14"/35.5 cm (or approximately 56 rows), beginning with a right-side row. Bind off.

Repeat three times for a total of four rectangular panels.

finishing

Weave in all loose ends with the tapestry needle.

With the right sides facing outwards, pin one of the long edges of one of the four rectangular panels to one of the side edges of the square panel. Make sure the stitches and rows are straight and that there's no stretching or puckering. Repeat this process with the three remaining edges of the square panel. Pin the short edges of the side panels to each other, making sure to line up the rows as well. For now, set aside the remaining square panel. With same yarn you used for rest of cover, work a single crochet around all the edges you've pinned together to attach those panels to each other and form a decorative edging. Remove pins one by one as you crochet.

Place this crocheted cover piece snugly over the top of the ottoman and turn it upside-down. The top panel has been knitted a bit smaller than the ottoman to ensure a proper fit. Place the remaining square panel on the bottom of the ottoman with the right side facing up and pin it evenly to the four rectangular side panels. Attach this square panel to the rectangular side panels using single crochet.

Now sit down, put your feet up, and relax!

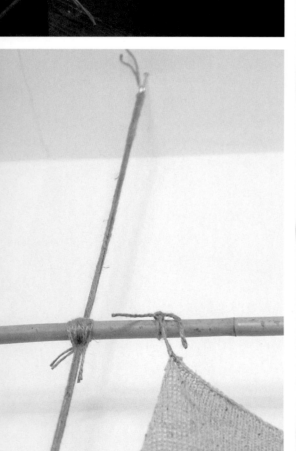

art wall hanging

I made this piece for my new home and hung it in a niche over a shelf holding votive candles and small rocks.

art wall hanging {experienced}

For this project, tweedy, rough yarn is stretched on bamboo poles, almost like an animal hide, with some rope for rustic appeal. My free-form version is knit in stockinette on small needles with dropped stitches, but the pattern here is more straightforward. Even though it has a great unstructured look, it is actually symmetrical. The only special stitches required are increases and decreases.

FINISHED MEASUREMENTS
(NOT INCLUDING BAMBOO ROD HANGING FRAME)

Approximately 25"/63.5 wide × 37"/94 cm long (see diagram)

YARN

5 skeins Suss Speckled (90% wool/10% cotton; 2 ounces/
57 grams; 114 yards/105 meters), color ash

NOTIONS

1 pair size 10¼"/ 6.5 mm needles (24" circular needles optional)
Knitting row counter (recommended)
Tapestry needle
1 roll natural jute twine 3-ply medium weight, 208 feet/64 meters
(available at most hardware stores)
2 bamboo rods; each 50"/127 cm long, 1"/2.5 cm in diameter
4 ceiling hooks, ¼"/1 cm diameter

GAUGE

16 stitches and 20 rows = 4"/10 cm in stockinette stitch

making the wall hanging

Divide the yarn into two balls. Cast on 10 stitches from one ball (Section B) and then cast on 10 stitches from the second ball on the same needle (Section A). You will have a total of 20 stitches on one needle from two balls. Section A will be on the right side of the needle when the knit side of the piece is facing you (see diagram). Work each section separately for the first 20 rows. By working both sections at the same time, you will create a symmetrical appearance.

Work from both balls in stockinette stitch (knit right-side rows, purl wrong-side rows), beginning with a right-side row. In Section A, increase one stitch at the beginning of every third row (Rows 3, 6, 9, and so on) and one stitch at the end of every row for 20 rows. In Section B, increase one stitch at the beginning of every row and at the end of every third row for 20 rows.

Starting with Row 21, join the two sections together. Start knitting Section A and continue knitting across Section B using the same ball of yarn you used for Section A. Work an increase at the beginning and end of this row. Cut off the yarn from the second ball and, using the tapestry needle, make a small knot and weave in the loose ends. You should now have 74 stitches on your needle (see diagram).

Continue working in stockinette, increasing one stitch at the beginning and end of every third row (Rows 24, 27, 30, and so on) until you have 60 rows total (40 rows from where you joined the two sections) and 100 stitches altogether.

Continue in stockinette stitch, decreasing one stitch at the beginning and end of every purl row 16 times (32 rows total). At the end of this section (Row 92), you will have 68 stitches altogether, and you are now halfway done!

Continue in stockinette stitch, increasing one stitch at the beginning and end of every purl row 16 times (32 rows total). You will now be on Row 124 and have 100 stitches.

Continue in stockinette stitch, decreasing one stitch at the beginning and end of every third row (Rows 127, 130, 133, and so on) until you have a total of 74 stitches (Row 163). Purl one row (Row 164).

Before you begin the next row (Row 165), prepare another ball of yarn. As in the beginning of this piece, you will be working from now on with two balls of yarn (see diagram). Start this row by decreasing one stitch and then knit 36 stitches from the ball you've been working from already (Section C). Then, taking yarn from the new ball, knit another 35 stitches (Section D) and decrease one stitch at the end of the row by knitting the last two stitches together. You may want to anchor the end of the new ball to the center of the knitted piece with a small knot. Weave in any loose ends with the tapestry needle.

Continue working in stockinette stitch. In Section C, decrease one stitch at the beginning of every third row (Rows 166, 169, 172, and so on) and one stitch at the end of every row for 20 rows. In Section D, decrease one stitch at the beginning of every row and at the end of every third row for 20 rows.

You should now have 10 stitches left in each section (Row 184). Knit one more row and bind off loosely on the next row.

increases and decreases

To increase stitches on a knit row: insert the right needle as if you were going to knit, wrap the yarn around the needle, and draw the loop of yarn through but *do not* remove the stitch from the left needle. Re-insert the right needle into the back of the same stitch, wrap the yarn around the needle and pull it through. Slip the stitch off the left needle.

To increase stitches on a purl row: insert the right needle as if you were going to purl, wrap the yarn around the needle, and draw the loop of yarn through but *do not* remove the stitch from the left needle. Re-insert the right needle into the back of the same stitch, wrap the yarn around the needle and pull it through. Slip the stitch off the left needle.

To decrease stitches on a purl row: purl two stitches together at the same time.

To decrease stitches on a knit row: knit two stitches together at the same time.

Weave in all loose ends with the tapestry needle.

Cut 8 lengths of the jute rope twine about 20"/51 cm each. Work one of these lengths of twine through a knit stitch and tie to each of the 8 points of the wall hanging (see diagram). Note: If you want, you can tie it in additional places, as I did in the photograph shown.

Screw two hooks in your ceiling about 30"/76 cm apart and about 4"/10 cm away from your wall. Screw two hooks into your floor at corresponding points in a straight vertical line from the ceiling hooks. Thread a length of twine approximately 2 yards/2 meters in length, fold it in half and thread it through one of the ceiling hooks and then thread the two ends through that loop (lark's head knot). Attach one of the bamboo rods to this twine at the desired height by wrapping the twine around the rod and tying it off. Do the same thing with the other ceiling hook. Cut off any excess bits of twine but don't worry too much about loose ends—they are part of the decorative charm of this fun wall hanging.

Cut two more lengths of twine about 4 yards/4 meters each, fold them in half, and attach them to the top bamboo rod with a lark's head knot. Attach the other bamboo rod to these lengths of twine in the same way about 50"/127 cm below the other rod, or whatever length you think looks right for your décor. These are your vertical anchor strings. Draw the bottom rod taut by taking two more lengths of twine, threading them through the floor hooks and tying them tightly around the bottom bamboo rod.

Tie the two top corner points of your knitted piece to the bamboo so the top of the piece is stretched flat. Tie the bottom and side corner points of the wall hanging to the bottom bamboo rod and the vertical anchor strings respectively, making sure that you pull the knitted piece to the appropriate tautness.

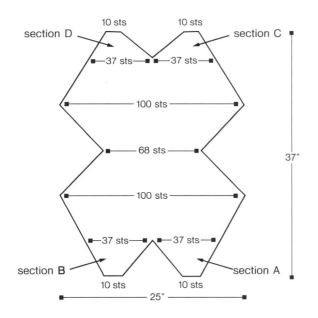

pastel
patchwork
throw

This romantic blanket is like a painting in an artist's palette of three summer garden colors. I've made at least a dozen of these as wedding gifts—for one special friend, I followed up with a miniature version when she had her first baby.

pastel patchwork throw {easy}

Knit three panels in stockinette stitch, then sew them together so the completed piece is asymmetrical. A crochet edge and tassels on each corner make it perfect for the bottom of your bed or to use as a throw for your TV couch. If you want an edgier feel, you could use camel, beige, and chocolate, or red, hot pink, and baby pink.

FINISHED MEASUREMENT

60"/152.5 cm wide × 60"/152.5 cm long

YARN

A: 8 skeins Suss Lux (40% cotton/40% polyamide/20% rayon; 2 ounces/54 grams; 56 yards/52 meters), color mauve

B: 8 skeins Suss Lux (40% cotton/40% polyamide/20% rayon; 2 ounces/54 grams; 56 yards/52 meters), color wildgrass

C: 8 skeins Suss Lux (40% cotton/40% polyamide/20% rayon; 2 ounces/54 grams; 56 yards/52 meters), color grey

D: 4 skeins Suss Natural (65% cotton/35% rayon; 2 ounces/ 57 grams; 70 yards/65 meters)

NOTIONS

1 pair size 10 (6mm) needles (24"/61 cm circular needles optional)

Tapestry needle

1 size G (4mm) crochet hook

Safety pins (optional)

GAUGE

12 stitches and 16 rows = 4"/10 cm in stockinette stitch

making the throw

Make two of Panel A and one of Panel B for a total of 3 panels.

panel a

With yarn A, cast on 60 stitches. Work in stockinette stitch (knit right-side rows and purl wrong-side rows) for 20"/51 cm, approximately 80 rows, beginning with a right-side row and ending with a wrong-side row.

Change color to yarn B and continue to work in stockinette stitch for 20"/51 cm, approximately 80 rows, ending with a wrong-side row.

Change color to yarn C and work in stockinette stitch for 20"/51 cm, approximately 80 rows, ending with a wrong-side row.

Bind off loosely.

panel b

With yarn B, cast on 60 stitches. Work in stockinette stitch for 20"/51 cm, approximately 80 rows, beginning with a right-side row and ending with a wrong-side row.

Change to yarn C and work in stockinette stitch for 20"/51 cm, approximately 80 rows, ending with a wrong-side row.

Change to yarn A and work in stockinette stitch for 20"/51 cm, approximately 80 rows, ending with a wrong-side row.

Bind off loosely.

finishing

Weave in all loose ends with the tapestry needle.

Line up the panels, right sides up, according to the diagram, placing Panel B in the middle of the two other panels. With the tapestry needle and two strands of yarn D, whipstitch together securely the right edge of Panel A to the left edge of Panel B. Then whipstitch the right edge of Panel B to the left edge of the other Panel A. Whipstitch using very small stitches to create a strong seam.

Once you've sewn the panels together, work a single crochet with yarn D stitch around all four edges of the blanket. The crochet edge makes the blanket strong and durable.

fringe

Cut yarn D into 300 lengths approximately 10"/25.5 cm long.

Attach fringe to the top and bottom edges of the throw. Using three lengths at a time, fold each group in half and use the crochet hook to pull the group through a hole in the crochet edging to form a loop. Then pull the yarn through the loop to make a fringe tassel. Space the tassels about 1"/2.5 cm apart. You should have about 50 fringe tassels on the top and bottom edges of the blanket.

grey	mauve	grey
wildgrass	grey	wildgrass
mauve	wildgrass	mauve

60"

20"

20"

60"

dining room
and kitchen

striped
seat covers

In my store, the small chairs around the table where I teach knitting are old and antique. I never tire of them, but I love to change their covers every six months or so, depending on my mood.

striped seat covers {intermediate}

If you find wonderful old chairs at the flea market, you can make them look new and match your home by knitting a seat cover. Knit fabric has a great stretch, so it's easy to fit almost any shape seat. Then you just staple it down. These are in cream and chocolate, classic enough colors to live with for a while. I made matching pillows for my couch, which gives the room a truly custom look.

SIZE

One size to fit seat 14"/35.5 cm wide × 15"/38 cm long (see diagram)

FINISHED MEASUREMENTS

Approximately 19"/48 cm long × 19"/48 cm wide (see diagram)

YARN

A: 5 skeins Suss Bomull (100% cotton; 4 ounces/114 grams; 190 yards/175 meters), color ecru

B: 2 skeins Suss Bunny (100% polyamide; 2 ounces/57 grams; 112 yards/103 meters), color chocolate

NOTIONS

1 pair size 7 (4.5 mm) needles

Tapestry needle

Staple gun and box of staples

4 seat cushions 14"/35.5 cm wide × 15"/38 cm long

GAUGE

17 stitches and 24 rows = 4"/10 cm in stockinette stitch

making the seat cover

With yarn A, cast on 82 stitches.

Work in stockinette stitch (knit right-side row and purl wrong-side rows) for 14 rows, beginning with a right-side row.

Work the following stripe pattern a total of 6 times.

Begin stripe pattern: Change to yarn B and knit one row. Purl the next row, decreasing one stitch at the beginning and end of the row. At the beginning of the row, decrease by purling two stitches and then use the left-hand needle to slip the first purled stitch over the second. At the end of the row, decrease by purling two stitches together at the same time.

To reduce the number of stray ends, do not cut yarn A when you work the thin stripes of yarn B. Let yarn A hang loose while you work the two rows of the yarn B stripe and then pick it up again to begin the next row of the stripe pattern.

Change to yarn A and work 12 rows in stockinette stitch.

You should now have 70 stitches and 98 rows. Work one more stripe with yarn B, remembering to decrease one stitch at the beginning and end of the purl row (68 stitches total). Work 14 more rows of yarn A in stockinette stitch (114 rows total). Your seat cushion cover should now measure approximately 19"/48 cm from the cast-on row and be approximately 16"/40.5 cm wide.

Bind off. Make three more seat covers.

finishing

Weave in all loose ends with the tapestry needle.

Center the seat cushion on the wrong side of the finished piece with the right side facing down on a flat, steady surface. Wrap the bottom edge of the knitted piece up around the wider straight edge (15"/38 cm) of the seat and secure it to the underside using a staple gun. Upholstery tacks will also work. Use the stripes in the knitted pattern to guide you in stapling the piece on straight.

To ensure a smooth finished product, pull the knitted piece over the straight edge opposite the one you just attached and staple that edge as well. Make sure the stripes in the knitted pattern are lying straight on the seat. Then staple the other two sides to the back of the seat cushion, folding the corners as if you were wrapping a package. Staple down any excess folds.

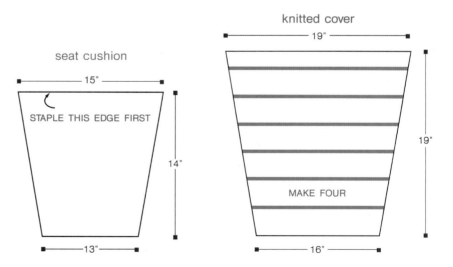

seat cushion

STAPLE THIS EDGE FIRST

15"

14"

13"

knitted cover

19"

19"

MAKE FOUR

16"

beaded
placemats

A set of placemats would make a cherished gift. Roll them together, wrap with a huge bow, and attach a handmade note card. Delicious!

beaded placemats {intermediate}

I love to set a beautiful table for dinner guests. These wood-beaded placemats in a rippled cotton texture make a versatile foundation. I keep the colors soft so napkins and other accessories can be bright for contrast. Don't be afraid to vary the edges from wood beads to crochet, fringe, or crystal beading.

FINISHED MEASUREMENTS

12"/30.5 cm wide ×19"/48 cm long

YARN

8 skeins Suss Cotton (100% cotton; 2$\frac{1}{2}$ ounces/71 grams; 118 yards/109 meters), color willow

NOTIONS

1 pair size 4 (3.5 mm) needles

Tapestry needle

1 size G (4 mm) crochet hook

Sewing needle and thread in complementary color

3 yards/3 meters of 1"/2.5 cm long beaded trim of your choice (available at craft and fabric stores)

GAUGE

18 stitches and 26 rows = 4"/10 cm in stockinette stitch

making the placemats

Cast on 54 stitches.

Work 14 rows in stockinette stitch (knit right-side rows and purl wrong-side rows), beginning with a right-side row.

Beginning with Row 15, work 16 rows in reverse stockinette stitch (purl right-side rows and knit wrong-side rows) for a total of 30 rows. To create the rippled effect of the placemat, you will work one purl row after another in the transition between stockinette stitch and reverse stockinette stitch.

Work 16 rows in stockinette stitch and 16 rows in reverse stockinette stitch (32-row pattern) twice (94 rows total). Work 16 rows of stockinette stitch (110 rows). Work 14 rows of reverse stockinette stitch (124 rows). The piece should measure 19"/48 cm.

Bind off stitches loosely.

Make three more placemats.

finishing

Weave in all loose ends with tapestry needle.

Work a single crochet using same yarn around all four edges.

Using the sewing needle and thread, attach beaded trim to the underside of the placemat on each 12"/30.5 cm side. Make sure that the stitches don't show on the front side of the placemat.

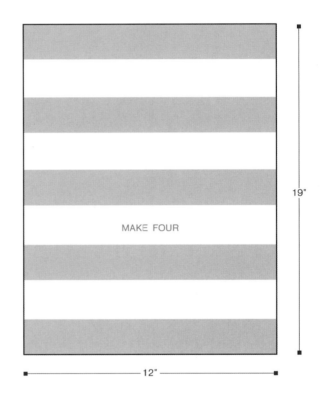

MAKE FOUR

19"

12"

chair covers with ribbon ties

These chair covers knit up in no time at all. Finishing may take a bit longer for this project than others, but the fabulous results will make it worth your while.

chair covers with ribbon ties

{ experienced }

I bought these simple wooden kitchen chairs at Ikea, the Swedish store where I used to shop with my parents as a little girl. The chairs needed a nice, deep cushion to make them more comfortable, but the ones I bought in cream cotton needed some spicing up. I began with the idea of a lush yarn spun from alpaca fur—oh so soft. Then I found a beautiful linen rayon ribbon to match. The ribbons are decorative, while the matte buttons help keep the cover in place.

SIZE

One size to fit seat cushion 19"/48 cm wide × 18"/45.5 cm

FINISHED MEASUREMENTS

Approximately 18"/45.5 cm wide × 32"/81 cm

Note: The size of the knitted chair cover is slightly smaller than the seat cushion to ensure a tight fit.

YARN

8 skeins Suss Brushed Alpaca (100% alpaca; 2 ounces/57 grams; 58 yards/54 meters), color natural

NOTIONS

1 pair size 10 (6mm) needles

Knitting row counter (recommended)

Tapestry needle

5 yards/4.5 meters linen organza ribbon, 3"/7.6 cm wide

Sewing needle and thread in matching color

Safety pins

2 khaki-colored cotton chair pad cushions with 100% polyester filling and 4 pre-tufted button indentations, approximately 19" wide × 18" long/48 cm × 45.5 cm

16 matching buttons, 1¼"/3 cm diameter

GAUGE

14 stitches and 20 rows = 4"/10 cm in stockinette stitch

making the chair cover

Cast on 24 stitches *loosely*.

Work in stockinette stitch (knit right-side row and purl wrong-side row) for 16 rows, beginning with a right-side row. Increase one stitch at the beginning and end of every row (instructions for increasing and decreasing are on page 48), for a total of 56 stitches. Continue working in stockinette stitch, increasing one stitch at the beginning and end of every purl row (Rows 18, 20, 22, and 24) for 8 rows (64 stitches total). Continue in stockinette stitch until piece measures 15"/38 cm from cast-on edge, approximately 75 rows, ending with a wrong-side row.

On the next two rows, bind off 6 stitches at the beginning of the row and work remaining stitches in stockinette stitch (52 stitches total).

Continue working in stockinette stitch for 10 rows.

On the next two rows, add 6 stitches at the beginning of the row and work remaining stitches in stockinette. To add new stitches, insert the right-hand needle into the space between the first two stitches on the left-hand needle. Pull the yarn through, making a loop, and place that loop back on the left-hand needle. Repeat this process until you have the desired number of stitches.

Continue working in stockinette stitch for 10"/25.5 cm, approximately 50 rows, or until piece measures 27"/68.5 cm from cast-on edge, approximately 135 rows. For the next 8 rows, decrease one stitch at the beginning and end of every other row for a total of 56 stitches. For the next 16 rows, decrease one stitch at the beginning and end of every row, for a total of 24 stitches. Bind off *loosely*.

Make two chair pad covers.

finishing

Weave in all loose ends with the tapestry needle.

Cut the ribbon into 40"/102 cm lengths. Turn each narrow edge of ribbon over $1/4$"/1 cm twice and hem using the sewing needle and thread. Do this for every ribbon.

Fold one of the lengths of ribbon in half and attach this folded, gathered edge to the rounded corner of the chair pad cushion with the sewing needle and thread. Before you attach the ribbon, place the cushion on the chair to make sure that the ribbons are in the right spot to tie them to the chair's back supports. Mark these spots with safety pins and sew on the ribbons securely.

After you've sewn the ribbons on the chair pad, fold the chair pad cover in half and whipstitch closed the small corner edges using the tapestry needle (see diagram).

Either whipstitch or use a vertical invisible join to sew together the first 5"/13 cm of both sides of the cover. To work an invisible join, line up all the knit stitches on the sides of the cushion. You may find it helpful to pin the pieces together with safety pins first. Turn the seat cushion until you are facing one of the side seams and the back edge (where the ribbons are attached) is facing away from you. Starting with the first stitch at the bottom of the panel on your left, insert the tapestry needle under the horizontal bar between the first and second stitches. Then insert the needle into the corresponding bar on the righthand piece.

Draw the pieces together so the two stitch halves resemble one complete knit stitch. Continue in this fashion alternating from the lefthand piece to the right. Leave the end loose as you work the first 5"/13 cm of the other side of the cushion.

Insert the chair pad into the knitted cover with the cast-on and bind-off edges meeting in the back between the attached ribbons. Use safety pins to hold the two halves together on the chair pad while you join them. Finish joining the sides together until you reach the ribbon ties. Whipstitch the ribbon ties to the chair pad cover and tie off your yarn.

Join the back seam between the ribbon ties. Using the tapestry needle and one strand of the yarn, you can either whipstitch the edges together or use a horizontal invisible join (see page 17), which will make the seam much less noticeable. Whichever stitch you use, you will find it helpful to safety pin the edges together first.

Weave in the loose ends.

Repeat the same process with the second chair pad.

To attach the buttons, use the tapestry needle and two strands of yarn. Knot one end of the yarn, insert the needle through one of the button indentations on one side of the cushion, pull it through to the other side, thread the needle through the button, and pull the needle through to the first side again. Pull the needle through to the other side of the chair pad again and wrap around the yarn shank of the button a few times. Pull the yarn through to the first side again before tying off. Repeat this process for all the buttons.

Tie the ribbons of your covered chair pads to your chairs, sit back and relax.

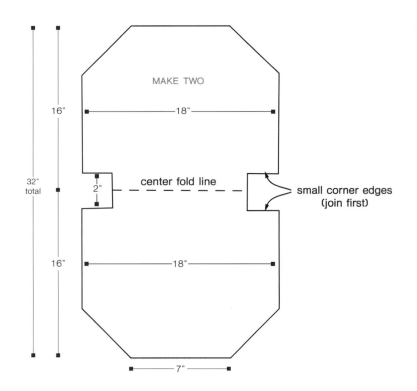

napkin holder
with button

I give a lot of dinner parties and have
so many different sets of linens, I'll be
knitting these napkin rings for a while!
Luckily, the Ultrasuede is thin, flat, and
very easy to work with.

napkin holder with button {easy}

My grandmother used to crochet dainty napkin rings in delicate mercerized cotton. They were perfect for her beautiful china. My table settings tend to be more casual, with pottery and stoneware, so I created a napkin ring in this rich, durable Ultrasuede. A garter stitch adds extra nubbiness. And since I collect buttons, I added the horn button to the design. These napkin rings don't take much time at all to knit, and I think a set of twelve is ideal. You can also knit them in different colors to match all your napkins and tablecloths.

SIZE

$2^1/2$"/6.5 cm in diameter when closed with button

FINISHED MEASUREMENTS

$2^1/4$"/5.5 cm wide × $7^1/2$"/19 cm long

YARN

1 skein Suss Ultrasuede (100% Ultrasuede; 4 ounces/114 grams; 70 yards/64 meters), color beige

NOTIONS

1 pair size 9 (5.5 mm) needles

Tapestry needle

4 2"/5 cm horn buttons

GAUGE

Approximately 12 stitches and 24 rows = 4"/10 cm in garter stitch

making the napkin holder

Cast on 7 stitches loosely. Knit all rows (garter stitch) until the holder measures approximately $6^1/4$"/16.5 cm.

On the next two rows, you will make the buttonhole. First, knit 2 stitches, bind off 3 stitches, and knit the remaining 2 stitches. On the next row, knit 2 stitches, make 3 stitches, and knit the remaining 2 stitches. To make the 3 new stitches, insert the right-hand needle into the space between the first two stitches on the left-hand needle. Pull the Ultrasuede through, making a loop, and place that loop back on the left-hand needle. Repeat this process two more times.

Continue knitting until the napkin holder is approximately 7¹/₂"/19 cm long, approximately 45 rows.

Bind off loosely. Make three more.

finishing

Weave in all loose ends with tapestry needle.

With the Ultrasuede, sew on the horn button securely approximately 1"/2.5 cm from the center of the edge of the napkin holder opposite the edge with the buttonhole.

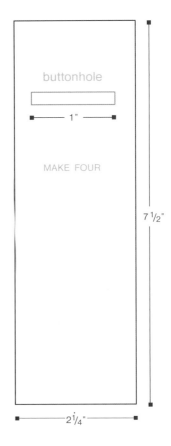

buttonhole

◄— 1" —►

MAKE FOUR

7¹/₂"

◄— 2¹/₄" —►

crystal table runner

My mother always put a runner on the table for holidays, and this one would work well for your special occasions or as a wedding gift.

crystal table runner {easy}

I have many beautiful natural linen tablecloths from Sweden, so I like to add soft color with a table runner. A typical Swedish pattern is knit in intarsia on each edge. You can decorate it with Austrian crystal beads or sequins—either way, it easily fits in with many tabletop concepts.

FINISHED MEASUREMENTS

Approximately 16"/40.5 cm wide × 92"/234 cm long

YARN

A: 6 skeins Suss Angora (70% angora/30% nylon; 1.5 ounces/ 43 grams; 246 yards/ 227 meters each), color aqua

B: 1 skein Suss Lurex (65% nylon/35% metallic; 1 ounce/29 grams; 225 yards/208 meters each), color gold

NOTIONS

1 pair size 9 (5.5 mm) needles

Tapestry needle

1 size G (4 mm) crochet hook

12 6 mm Austrian crystal beads in matching color

GAUGE

18 stitches and 24 rows = 4"/10 cm in stockinette stitch

making the table runner

Using a double strand of yarn A, cast on 72 stitches.

Work in stockinette stitch (knit right-side rows and purl wrong-side rows) for 12 rows.

Begin squares pattern: Using the Fair Isle method, join a double strand of yarn B and knit 3 stitches while carrying yarn A along the back of the piece; knit 3 stitches in yarn A while carrying yarn B in the back. Alternate like this every 3 stitches to the end of the row.

For the next row, purl 3 stitches with yarn A and alternate every 3 stitches with yarn B until the end of the row.

Repeat this pattern for two more rows until the squares are 4 rows high. Cut ends of yarn B leaving a short tail. There will be 12 squares of each color.

Work four rows of stockinette stitch in yarn A.

Begin second squares pattern: Using the Fair Isle method of carrying yarn along the back of your work, knit 3 stitches with yarn A. Knit 3 stitches with yarn B, and alternate every 3 stitches to the end of the row.

For the next row, purl 3 stitches with yarn B, then 3 stitches with yarn A, alternate until the end of the row. Repeat this pattern until the squares are 4 rows high. Cut the ends of yarn B leaving a short tail. There will be 12 squares of each color in a checkerboard-style pattern with the first row of squares.

Continue in stockinette stitch with yarn A until piece measures approximately 88 inches, approximately 528 rows, ending with a wrong-side row.

For the next 12 rows, repeat the two squares patterns from above. Knit 12 rows of stockinette stitch in yarn A and then bind off loosely.

finishing

Weave in all loose ends with the tapestry needle.

Using a double strand of yarn A, single crochet a border around all four sides of table runner.

Using one strand of yarn A, sew six crystal beads at regular intervals across the rows between the gold squares (see photograph).

Using two strands of yarn A, cut 64 lengths of yarn 14"/35.5 cm long. Place two 14"/35.5 cm lengths together and fold them in half to form a loop. Using the crochet hook, pull the loop through a space in the edging and pull the ends of the yarn through the loop. Tighten the loop to form the fringe. Starting at the edge, place fringe across the narrow end of the table runner approximately 1"/2.5 cm apart.

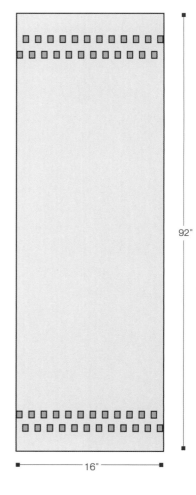

92"

16"

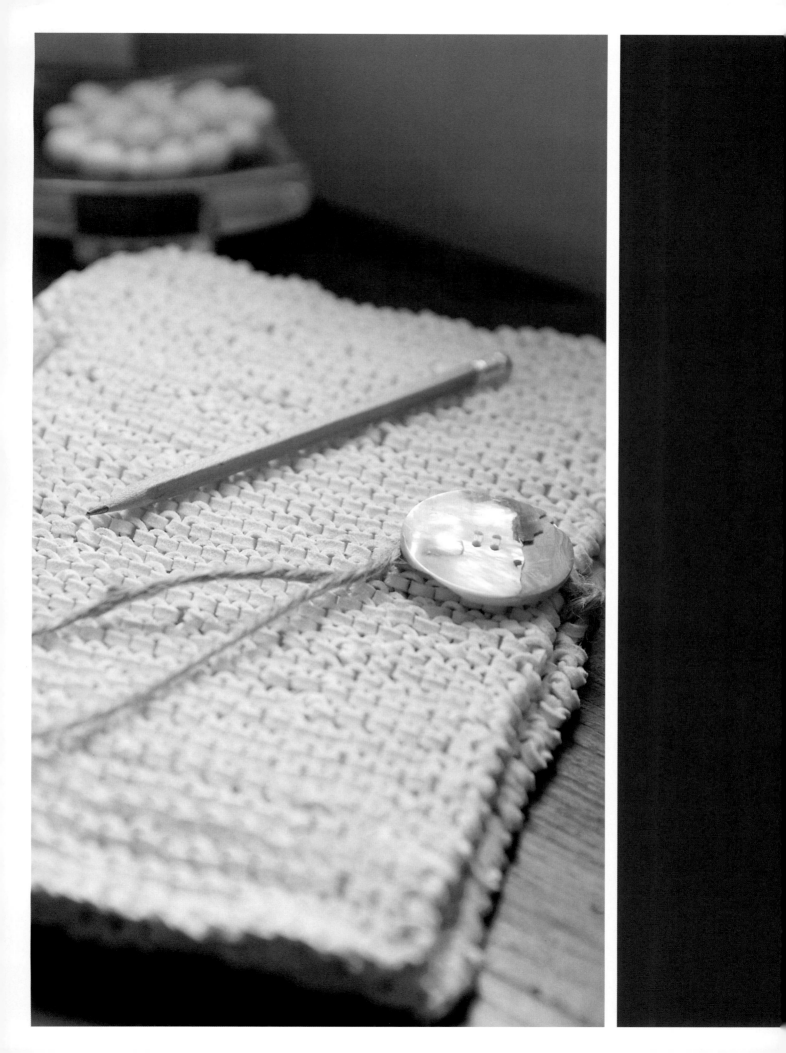

knitted guestbook

This knitted book makes a great piece on your table for guests to share their thoughts on the spirit of an evening dining at your house.

knitted guestbook {easy}

This cover is simply knitted in garter stitch to keep its stiffness and then bound into a guestbook, a journal, or whatever else you want it to be. I love to use that thick, natural-colored paper with flowers or leaves pressed into it. For a festive variation, you could knit it in red and have people write in gold ink.

SIZE

One size to fit paper sheets 7"/18 cm wide × 10"/25.5 cm long

FINISHED MEASUREMENTS

7¹/₂"/19 cm wide × 11"/28 cm long

YARN

1 skein Suss Ultrasuede (100% Ultrasuede; 4 ounces/114 grams; 70 yards/64 meters), color cream

NOTIONS

1 pair size 8 (5 mm) needles

Tapestry needle

Sewing needle and matching thread

1³/₄"/5 cm abalone button

2 yards natural jute twine 3-ply medium weight (available at most hardware stores)

1 size G (4 mm) crochet hook

12 sheets high-quality notepaper cut into 7" × 10" pieces, or as many sheets as you desire (for archival quality, choose acid-free paper)

Paper punch

GAUGE

15 stitches and 24 rows = 4"/10 cm in garter stitch

making the guestbook

Cast on 28 stitches loosely.

Work in garter stitch (knit every row) for 11"/28 cm, or approximately 66 rows.

Bind off stitches loosely.

Make two.

finishing

Weave in all ends with the tapestry needle.

Using sewing needle and thread, attach abalone button on 1¹/₄"/3 cm from the center of the outside edge of the front cover, about 5¹/₂"/14 cm from the bottom.

To make the button tie closure, cut a 30"/76 cm piece of jute twine. Fold the twine in half and, using the crochet hook, pull a loop through edge of back cover, 5¹/₂"/14 cm up from the bottom. Pull ends through loop. Make sure the button tie closure is lined up with the abalone button.

To bind the book, punch four holes in each sheet of paper: the first hole should be about 1"/2.5 cm below the top of the paper and ¹/₂"/1 cm from the edge. The second hole should be about 2"/5 cm below the top hole. Repeat for the bottom binding, punching the third and fourth holes ¹/₂"/1 cm from the edge at 1"/2.5 cm and 3"/7.5 cm from the bottom. To assemble the book, center the paper stack evenly between the front and back covers. With the tapestry needle and the natural jute twine, insert the needle through the top cover at the same place as the first hole in the paper, thread it through the paper and the bottom cover. Loop around the first two paper holes twice and finish with a knot. Repeat for the third and fourth paper holes.

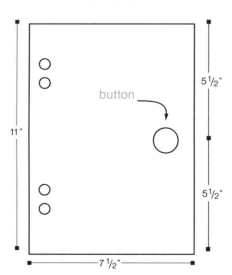

front cover

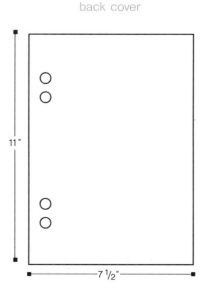

back cover

two-tone kitchen curtains

The windows in the kitchen of my new house are wonderful, but they let the neighbors look right in. I needed something to block their view and to add a decorative touch to a very simple room. Since I grow orchids, my favorite flowers, on the windowsill, a mix of soft-colored yarns seemed like just the right touch.

two-toned kitchen curtains

{intermediate}

These curtains are easy to make, and it's the tweediness of the yarn that makes them interesting. As I stand at the sink, the curtains come to right below my nose, and I tied them with a cute ribbon tie bow on top. My favorite thing about them, though, is the hand-crocheted trim, which reminds me of my grandmother. She used to crochet little white curtains for every room in the house!

FINISHED MEASUREMENTS

34"/86 cm wide × 12"/30.5 cm long (including decorative edge)

YARN

5 skeins Suss Twisted (100% cotton; 2.5 ounces/71 grams; 108 yards/98 meters), color salmon/natural

NOTIONS

1 pair size 8 (5 mm) circular needles, 24"/61 cm long

Tapestry needle

1 size G (4 mm) crochet hook

9 yards/9 meters of 1"/2.5 cm wide twill tape

Sewing needle and thread in complementary color

Note: This list of materials is for two curtain panels.

GAUGE

16 stitches and 24 rows = 4"/10 cm in stockinette stitch

making the kitchen curtain

Cast on 136 stitches.

Work in stockinette stitch (knit right-side rows, purl wrong-side rows) for 10"/25.5 cm, approximately 60 rows, ending with a wrong-side row. Bind off loosely.

Repeat to make a second kitchen curtain.

finishing

Weave in all loose ends with the tapestry needle.

Fold over the top edge of the curtain approximately 1"/2.5 cm and whipstitch to the back of the piece so that the seam is not visible on the front of curtain.

Single crochet around the other three sides of the panel. To create picot edge, start at one edge of the bottom of the panel, chain 3 stitches and begin fantail edging pattern in the hole of the second single crochet edging stitch.

fantail edge pattern

Triple crochet (yarn over two times, insert hook, yarn over, pull through stitch and then pull through 2 loops three times), chain 3, insert hook in the first of the 3 chain stitches and pull yarn through this hole and loop on hook, chain 1. Repeat this pattern four more times through the same hole in the curtain's edging.

Chain 1 again. Skip the next 2 single crochets on the curtain's edging and, inserting needle in the third single crochet, chain 2 loosely, skip 1 single crochet edging stitch, and begin fantail pattern again. You will have approximately 14 fantails across the bottom of your panel.

for curtain ties

Cut the twill tape into seven 24"/61 cm segments. Fold each in half and sew to the back of the curtain at approximately 5"/12.5 cm intervals starting at the very end of curtain so it will hang evenly. Be careful that your stitches don't go all the way through to the front side of the panel. Tie knots at each of the tape ends.

Repeat this process for the second panel.

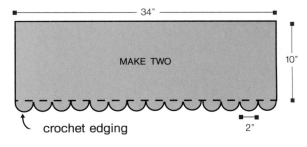

tote bag

This tote is perfect for when you just need to pick up a carton of milk or a loaf of bread.

tote bag {intermediate}

Try this bag for your quick errands instead of bringing home yet another plastic bag that isn't good for the environment. Knitted in durable cotton, it has sturdy Ultrasuede handles and a lining that you can make out of any tightly woven fabric. I picked an embroidered fabric; you could also try linen.

SIZE

18"/45.5 cm × 12"/30 cm × 5$\frac{1}{2}$"/14 cm

FINISHED MEASUREMENTS

Front and Back Panels: 18"/45.5 cm wide × 12"/30 cm long

Gusset: 5$\frac{1}{2}$"/14 cm × 42"/106 cm

Handles: 2$\frac{1}{2}$"/6.5 cm wide × 16$\frac{1}{2}$"/42 cm long

YARN

A: 7 skeins Suss Natural (65% cotton/35% rayon; 2 ounces/
57 grams; 76 yards/70 meters)

B: 1 ball Suss Perle Variegated (100% cotton; 2 ounces/57 grams;
256 yards/236 meters), color northwood

C: 3 skeins Suss Ultrasuede (100% ultrasuede; 4 ounces/
114 grams; 70 yards/64 meters), color beige

NOTIONS

1 pair size 8 (5 mm) needles

1 pair size 9 (5.5 mm) needles

Large tapestry needle

Quilting pins or T-pins

1 size G (4 mm) crochet hook

4 large buttons approximately 1"/4 cm in diameter

2 metal snap fasteners $\frac{7}{8}$"/2 cm in diameter

$\frac{3}{4}$ yard your choice matching fabric

Sewing needle and thread in off-white color

GAUGE

Front/Back Panels: 13 stitches and 18 rows = 4"/10 cm with one strand of yarn A and one strand of yarn B in stockinette stitch with size 9 needles

Gusset: 12 stitches and 16 rows = 4"/10 cm with two strands of yarn A in stockinette stitch with size 8 needles

Handles: 12 stitches and 24 rows = 4"/10 cm with one strand of yarn C in garter stitch with size 9 needles

making the tote bag

front panel

With one strand of yarn A and one strand of yarn B, cast on 60 stitches with size 9 needles. Work in stockinette stitch (knit right-side rows, purl wrong-side rows) for 54 rows. Bind off.

back panel

Repeat instructions for Front Panel.

gusset

With two strands of yarn A, cast on 17 stitches with size 8 needles. The smaller needles and tighter gauge will provide solidity and structure to the tote bag.

Work in stockinette stitch until the piece measures 42"/106 cm, approximately 168 rows, ending with a wrong-side row. Be sure that the total length of the strip equals the length of the left, bottom, and right edges of the Front/Back Panels.

Bind off.

handles

With yarn C and size 9 needles, cast on 8 stitches.

Work in garter stitch (knit every row) for 16$\frac{1}{2}$"/42 cm, approximately 99 rows.

Bind off loosely. Make two handles.

finishing

Weave in ends with the tapestry needle.

Pin the long edge of the Gusset to the right, bottom, and left edges of the Front Panel. Make sure that the top edges meet evenly. You may want to use extra pins to help ease the straight strip around the corner of the panel. Using the tapestry needle and yarn A, sew the pinned edges together.

Repeat the same process to attach the Back Panel to the Gusset.

Cut a length of yarn A about 2 yards/1.8 meters long and, using the tapestry needle or the crochet hook, attach it to one of the inside (wrong side) corners of the bag with a small knot. Turn the bag right-side out. Draw the yarn through with the crochet hook and work a single crochet across one of the knitted rows of the Gusset from one corner of the Front Panel to the corresponding corner of the Back Panel (see photograph). Repeat this single crochet on the other side of the tote bag. This will provide definition and shape to the bottom of the bag.

With one strand of yarn A and one strand of yarn B, crochet two rows of single crochet around the top edge of the tote bag.

Using the darning needle and the off-white thread, attach the snap fasteners to the each side of the Gusset near the top of the bag about 1"/2.5 cm from the top and 1"/2.5 cm from the sides.

lining

Assembling the lining is similar to constructing the bag. Cut the fabric into three pieces: two pieces 19"/48 cm × 13"/33 cm (front and back lining panel), and one piece 6$\frac{1}{2}$"/16.5 cm × 43"/109 cm (gusset lining). With the right sides facing each other pin the long edge of the gusset to three sides of the front lining panel and, using the sewing needle and thread, sew the two pieces together with a $\frac{1}{2}$"/1 cm seam all the way around. With the right sides facing each other, do the same with the back lining panel.

Insert this fabric lining "bag" into the knitted totebag. Fold over the top edge of the lining approximately $\frac{1}{2}$"/1 cm, and pin it into place at the edge of the line of single crochet. Using the sewing needle and the off-white thread, whipstitch the lining securely to the inside of the knitted totebag. Make sure your stitches aren't visible from the outside of the totebag.

handles

Using the tapestry needle, attach the handles to the bag using yarn C and the four large buttons. The centers of the buttons should be about 1$\frac{1}{2}$"/4 cm from the top crocheted edge of the bag and approximately 5"/13 cm from the side/bottom panel. Sew the buttons all the way through the handle, the knitted piece, and the lining, and knot on the inside. Tack down the handle at the bottom corners and the points where the handle intersects with the crocheted edge.

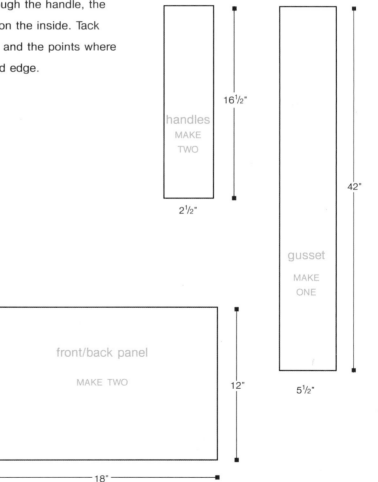

handles
MAKE TWO

16$\frac{1}{2}$"

2$\frac{1}{2}$"

gusset
MAKE ONE

42"

front/back panel

MAKE TWO

12"

18"

5$\frac{1}{2}$"

basketweave rug

The variegated basketweave can stand up to kitchen wear and tear, plus it doesn't show dirt. That was important in my kitchen because the kitties are always hovering around the sink waiting for scraps of leftovers.

basketweave rug {easy}

What is it about a kitchen? Each time I move, no matter how big or beautiful any of the other rooms are, it's the kitchen that becomes my favorite place. It's warm and cozy, and great things are happening in there! My current kitchen is all-natural in color with silver appliances, so I wanted a little kitchen rug for texture and softness. Of course, you could knit it larger for another room, or make it out of Ultrasuede. It's all up to your own imagination.

FINISHED MEASUREMENTS

24"/61 cm wide × 36"/91.5 cm long

YARN

A: 6 skeins Suss Coolaid (85% acrylic/15% wool; 2 ounces/
57 grams; 90 yards/83 meters), color honey

B: 3 skeins Suss Spacedye (100% cotton; 4 ounces/114 grams;
188 yards/174 meters), color earthtone

NOTIONS

1 pair size 11/ 8 mm needles (24"/61 cm circular needles
recommended)
Large tapestry needle

GAUGE

13 stitches and 16 rows = 4"/10 cm in basketweave pattern

making the rug

With a double strand of yarn A, cast on 80 stitches.

Work in a basketweave pattern as follows

Rows 1, 3, and 5: Knit 4, purl 4, and repeat until the end of the row.

Rows 2 and 4: Purl 4, knit 4, and repeat until the end of the row.

Change to a double strand of yarn B.

Rows 6,7, 9, and 11: Purl 4, knit 4, and repeat until the end of the row.

Rows 8 and 10: Knit 4, purl 4, and repeat until the end of the row.

Change to a double strand of yarn A.

Row 12: Knit 4, purl 4, and repeat until the end of the row.

Work basketweave pattern a total of 12 times, for 144 rows.

Note: For a sturdy edge with fewer loose ends, work the two strands of yarn A together with yarn B for the first stitch of every row that begins with a purl stitch. When working a row that begins with a knit stitch, slip the first stitch as if you were going to knit (knitwise) to create a smooth edge.

finishing

Bind off in the basketweave pattern. Weave in all loose ends with tapestry needle.

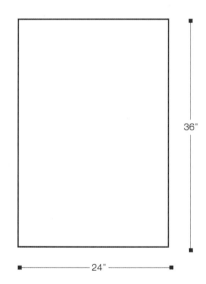

embroidered vase cover

Everyone seems to have a stash of plain glass vases from florists taking up space in the back of a cupboard. I experimented with my extras, covering one in a simple garter stitch knit, and then kept going with embroidery based on a motif from an old 1930s tablecloth.

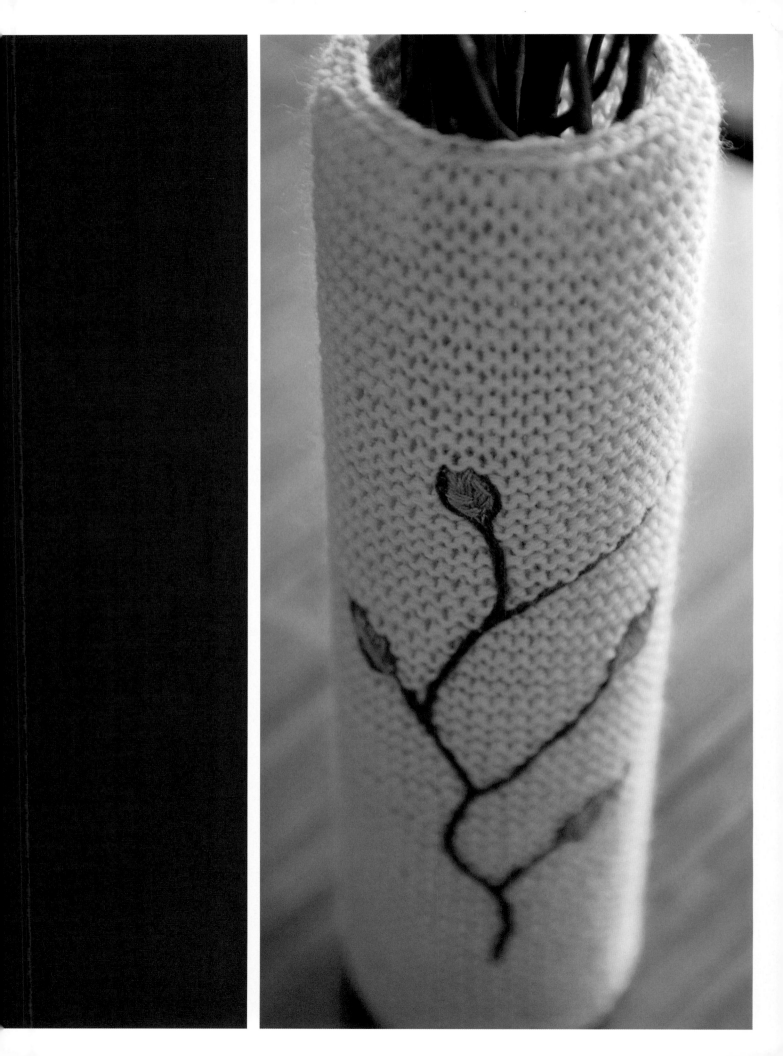

embroidered vase cover {intermediate}

The embroidery on this cover gives it a vintage feel and turns the vase into a piece of art. I keep this special vase in my guestroom. By using green and brown, the design will always match any arrangement I choose. You could also experiment with other embroidery fibers.

SIZE

One size to fit vase 5"/13 cm in diameter, 15 1/2"/39.5 cm tall

FINISHED MEASUREMENTS

16"/40.5 cm wide × 15 1/2"/ 39.5 cm

YARN

A: 4 skeins Suss Ull (100% wool; 2 ounces/57 grams; 215 yards/198 meters), color aran

B: 1 ball Suss Perle Cotton (100% cotton; 2 ounces/57 grams; 256 yards/236 meters), color okra

C: 1 ball Suss Perle Cotton (100% cotton; 2 ounces/57 grams; 256 yards/236 meters), color gold

NOTIONS

1 pair size 9 (5.5 mm) needles (16"/40.5 cm circular or double-pointed needles optional)

Tapestry needle

1 size G (4 mm) crochet hook

1 cylindrical clear glass vase, 5"/13 cm in diameter, 15 1/2"/39.5 cm tall

GAUGE

18 stitches and 32 rows = 4"/10 cm in garter stitch

making the vase cover

With two strands of yarn A, cast on 72 stitches. Work in garter stitch (knit every row) until piece measures 15$^1/_2$"/39.5 cm, approximately 124 rows, the height of the vase.

Bind off loosely.

If you choose to use circular needles or double pointed needles, make sure to mark the beginning of the rows with a stitch marker. In order to get the look of garter stitch, you will need to work in stockinette stitch (knit right-side rows, purl wrong-side rows). With this technique, you will not have a seam to join at the end.

finishing

Weave in all loose ends using the tapestry needle.

Thread two strands of yarn B in the tapestry needle. Follow the embroidery design pattern using chain stitches to outline the stems and the edges of the leaves (see diagram). The bottom of the leaf design should begin about 3"/8 cm from the bottom, and in the center of the rectangular piece so it will be on the opposite side of the vase cover from the seam. With two strands of yarn C, fill in the leaves with satin stitch, working outward from an imaginary line through the center of each leaf.

With a tapestry needle and yarn A, work in a vertical join along the side edges to form a tube. With two strands of yarn A, work a single crochet edge around the top edge of the vase cover.

Place the cover over the vase and fill it with your favorite flowers.

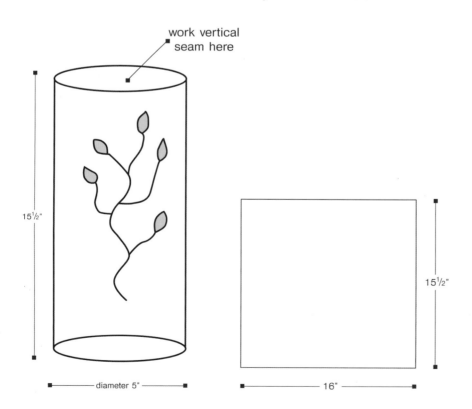

work vertical
seam here

15$^1/_2$"

diameter 5"

15$^1/_2$"

16"

bedroom
and bath

alpaca
lampshades

Lighting in the bedroom needs to be just right—warm, soft, and flattering, yet good for reading in bed. The lamp itself must be able to fit on the night-stand. For our bedroom, I thought a round lamp would work well because of its short lampshade. The soft alpaca yarn lets the light shine through and gives the room a glow.

alpaca lampshades {intermediate}

A shade in this fawn color creates intimate lighting for romantic moments. The rib pattern is classic and complements any decor.

FINISHED MEASUREMENTS

25"/63.5 cm × 14"/35.5 cm

YARN

6 skeins Suss Alpaca (100% alpaca; 2 ounces/57 grams; 163 yards/150 meters), color fawn

NOTIONS

1 pair size 10$^1/_2$ (6.5 mm) needles (24"/61 cm circular needles recommended)

1 stitch marker (recommended if you use circular needles)

Tapestry needle

2 lampshades: 8"/20 cm in diameter, 9"/23 cm tall

3 yards beading cord elastic, $^1/_2$"

1 safety pin

GAUGE

14 stitches and 16 rows = 4"/10 cm in rib pattern

making the lampshade

Cast on 88 stitches.

Work in a four-by-four rib (knit 4 stitches, purl 4 stitches), and repeat to the end of the row for 14"/35.5 cm, or approximately 56 rows.

Bind off stitches loosely following the rib pattern.

Note: This pattern may also be worked with 16"/41 cm or 24"/61 cm circular needles. Cast on 88 stitches as above and work in a four-by-four rib pattern. Make sure you place a stitch marker, or tie a piece of contrasting yarn, between the first and last stitch so your first row does not become twisted. When your piece measures 14"/35.5 cm (approximately 56 rows), bind off loosely following the rib pattern. You will not need to follow the seaming instructions below. Make two lampshades.

finishing

Weave in all loose ends with the tapestry needle.

Fold each long edge over 1$^1/_4$"/3 cm towards wrong side, and pin down with sewing pins. Whipstitch this seam using the tapestry needle and yarn, making sure that stitches are not visible on right side. Make sure the top and bottom seams are wide enough to allow you to thread the elastic through the channels.

Turn the piece over so the right side is facing outward and fold so that the short (cast-on and bind-off) edges meet. Use an invisible join (described on page 17), or whipstitch the two edges together, working between the seamed channel you have sewn down the long sides of the fabric. Leave the inside, or wrong side, of these channels open for the time being, as you will need these openings to thread elastic through the top and bottom of the finished lampshade. You may want to use safety pins to hold the edges together while you join them.

Repeat as follows: insert the needle knitwise into the same first stitch on the cast-on edge, and then insert the needle purlwise into the second stitch on the cast-on edge. Next, insert the needle purlwise into the first stitch on the bind-off edge, and then insert the needle knitwise into the second stitch on the bind-off edge. Repeat this process until you reach the final stitch before the seamed channel on the other long side, pulling the yarn tight every few stitches. The joining seam should be nearly invisible. With the tapestry needle, weave in any loose ends.

Cut the elastic in half. Attach the end of one half to one of the large safety pins. Thread the safety pin through the top channel, taking care to hold on to the other end of the elastic. Pin the two ends of the elastic together. Repeat this process on the bottom channel.

Test the size of the finished piece by fitting it over the lampshade. The cover should fit snugly over the lampshade but should also be loose enough that you can take it on and off for cleaning. The elastic should be tight enough to hold the piece in place. For the top channel, remove the safety pin and tie the two ends of the elastic together to give the piece the desired circumference. Repeat for the bottom channel. Take the piece off the lampshade and stitch up the top and bottom channel openings.

Stretch the lampshade cover over the lampshade and adjust it so it lies smoothly and the stitches line up vertically. Attach your lampshade to your lamp, turn on the light, and enjoy!

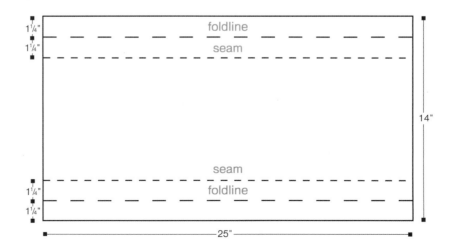

swedish bed canopy

In Sweden, a piece like this is a very popular way of creating a canopy over your guest bed, a sofa, or even a window seat. The silhouette is typically Swedish, and I love its cozy sophistication.

swedish bed canopy {intermediate}

I chose a neutral shade for this canopy so it would blend easily with any color scheme. Although it does takes some time to knit with small needles, the assembly is fast. All you need is a bamboo rod or wooden pole and some rope or leather string. Create your own private little world, and you'll feel like you are going off to paradise.

FINISHED MEASUREMENTS

Approximately 32"/81 cm wide × 180"/457 cm long

YARN

8 skeins Suss Ultrasoft (40% viscose/30% alpaca/20% acrylic/ 10% nylon; 1.5 ounces/42 grams; 204 yards/188 meters), color taupe

NOTIONS

1 pair size 11 (8 mm) circular knitting needles, 24"/61 cm long

Tapestry needle

Size 6 crochet hook

1 bamboo rod, 1"/2.5 cm in diameter and 36"/91 cm long

1 ball of twine

2 ceiling hooks

GAUGE

14 stitches and 16 rows = 4"/10 cm in stockinette stitch

making the canopy

Cast on 114 stitches.

Work in stockinette stitch (knit right-side rows and purl wrong-side rows) until piece measures 180"/457 cm, or desired length.

Bind off loosely.

finishing

Weave in ends using the tapestry needle. Work a single crochet around all four edges of the rectangular piece.

To create a channel for the bamboo hanging rod, fold the canopy in half and sew a seam approximately 3"/8 cm from the edge of the fold. You can use a sewing machine to do this or you may sew this seam by hand using a running stitch and a strand of yarn or a complementary color of sewing thread.

Hang the bamboo rod from the ceiling above your bed using two ceiling hooks placed about 30"/76 cm apart parallel with the center of the head of the bed (see diagram). Be creative with your choice of hardware and string to match your current décor. Cut two pieces of twine approximately 56"/142 cm long, or whatever length you desire so your canopy will hang at the height you want it to. Make two large loops at either end of the lengths of twine. Attach one loop of each piece of twine to each of the two ceiling hooks.

Thread the bamboo rod through the channel in the center of the canopy, and then thread both ends of the rod through the remaining loops in the twine. Make sure that the bamboo rod is balanced evenly at both ends. Let both halves of the canopy fall loosely over the sides of your bed.

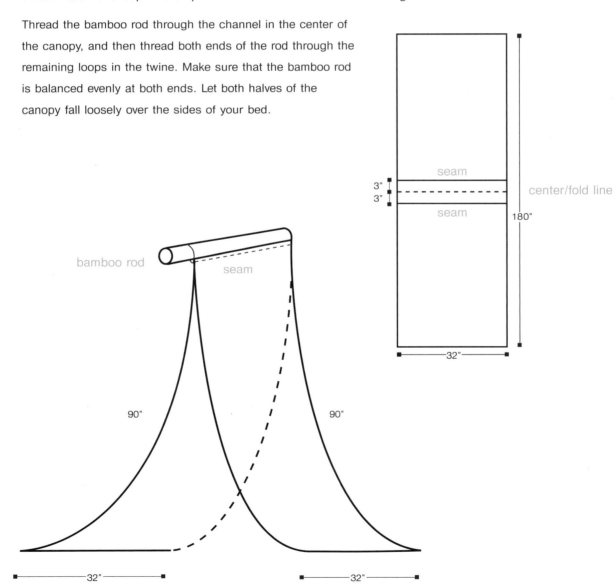

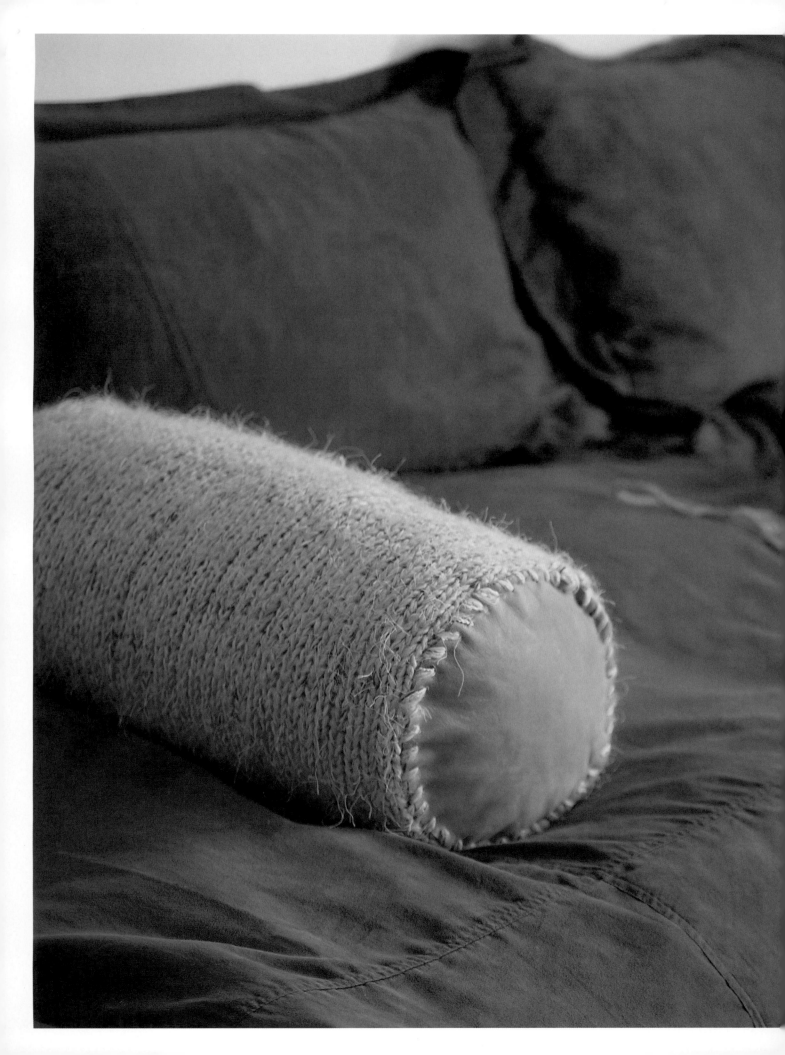

fantasy pillows

Pillows are all over my house, but this shape is one of my favorites—I think it's cool. I first saw pillows like these in a Moroccan restaurant, where they were used as armrests.

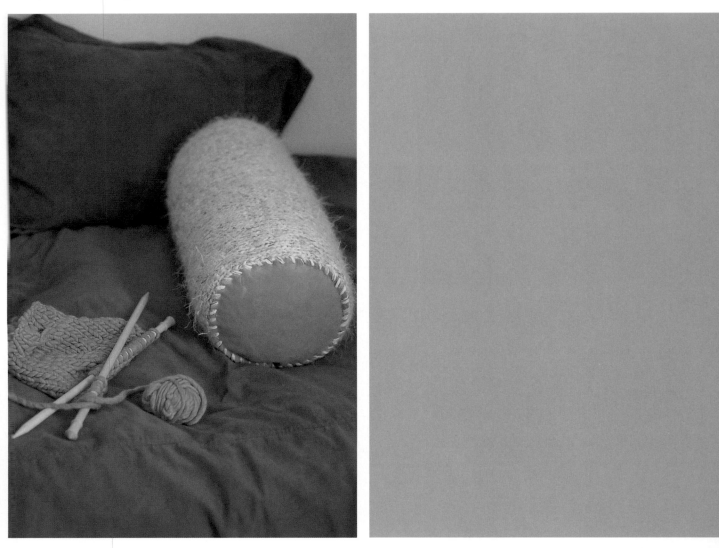

fantasy pillows {intermediate}

I put one of these pillows behind my head when I watch TV. Because it's round, it relieves tension in the neck, but of course, it's a decorative pillow first and foremost. Made in a mix of my exclusive yarns and finished off with leather or Ultrasuede circles, natural felt, or crochet, they fit in anywhere in the house.

SIZE

One size to fit bolster pillow measuring 9"/23 cm in diameter and 20"/51 cm wide

FINISHED MEASUREMENTS

20"/51 cm wide × 28"/72 cm long

YARN

9 skeins Suss Fantasy (50% cotton/15% mohair/10% viscose/10% nylon/10% polyester/5% wool; 4 ounces/114 grams; 50 yards/46 meters), color green moss

NOTIONS

1 pair size 13 (9 mm) needles

Large tapestry needle

2 bolster pillows approximately 9"/23 cm in diameter and 20"/51 cm wide

Several safety pins (recommended)

Leather or Ultrasuede (see note below for specifications)

Leather punch

Note: This list of materials is enough to make two bolster pillow covers. You can purchase similar bolster pillows at most home furnishing stores. If you want to make one yourself, use a neutral-colored, sturdy fabric and a pillow form or the 100% polyester stuffing available at fabric and craft stores. You should be able to find leather or Ultrasuede at your local fabric or craft store as well. You will need enough to make four circles 9"/23 cm in diameter. You can purchase either four squares of leather at least 9"/23 cm × 9"/23 cm or $1/4$ yard of Ultrasuede at least 36"/91 cm wide.

GAUGE

9 stitches and 13 rows = 4"/10 cm in stockinette stitch

making the pillow

Cast on 45 stitches.

Work in stockinette stitch (knit right-side rows, purl wrong-side rows) until piece measures 28"/72 cm long, approximately 92 rows, ending with a wrong-side row.

Bind off.

Make two.

finishing

To join the piece together in a tube shape, start by folding the cover over with the right side facing outward and the cast-on and bind-off edges meeting. Use an invisible join (see page 17) or whipstitch the two edges together. To make stitching easier, you may want to use safety pins or waste knots to hold the edges together while you join them.

Cut the leather or Ultrasuede into four circles 9"/23 cm in diameter and punch 42 holes around the perimeter of the circle about $1/2$"/1 cm from the edge of the circle and $1/2$"/1 cm apart. Insert the bolster pillow into the tubular casing of the knitted piece and place one of the leather circles on the end of the pillow. Using a tapestry needle and yarn, whipstitch the leather piece to the knitted cover using the holes you've punched into the leather. Attach the other leather piece to the other end of the bolster pillow.
Finish the second pillow in the same way.

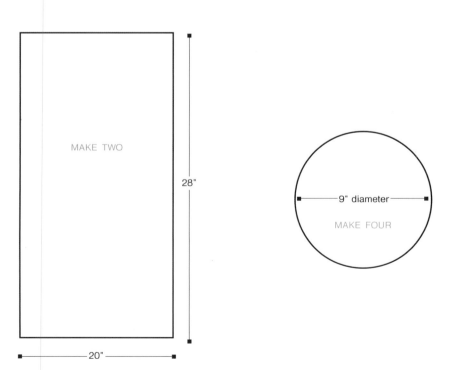

MAKE TWO

28"

20"

9" diameter

MAKE FOUR

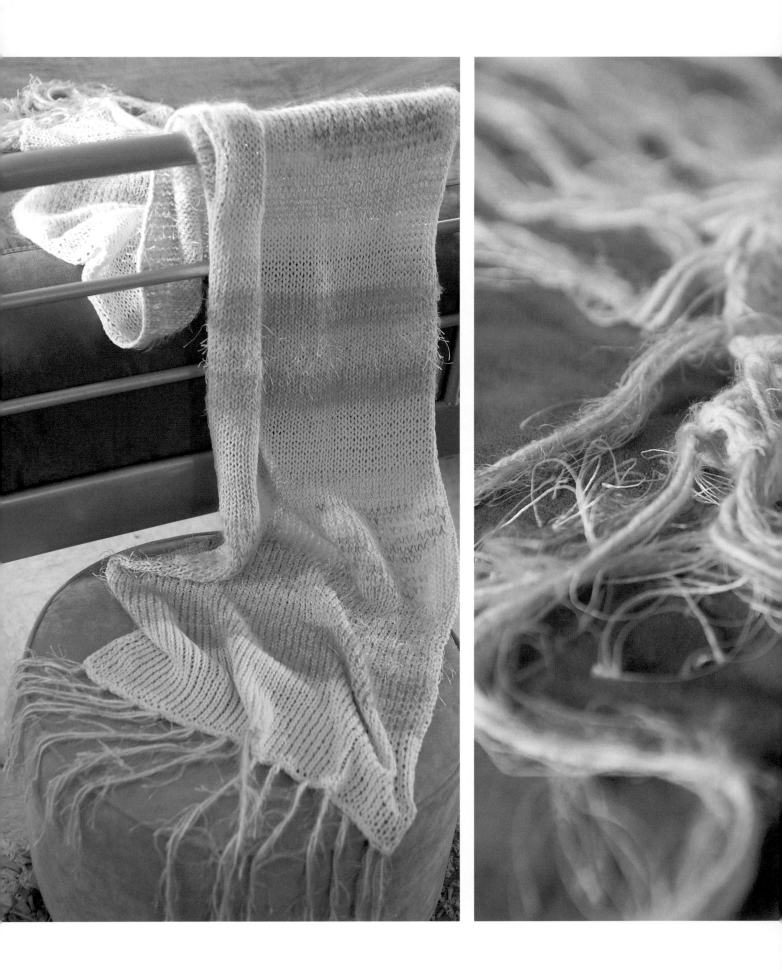

multi-yarn shawl

The inspiration for this cozy yet sophisticated shawl comes from my grandmother. In Sweden, she was always crocheting them for us to have over our shoulders in the cold winters while we curled up to watch TV. I've been making shawls ever since then, usually to give to someone.

multi-yarn shawl {intermediate}

This shawl is very easy to knit, but the mix of yarn gives it flair and adds character to a chair or couch when you're not using it—you could even wear it for an evening out. When my husband and I share a glass of wine in front of our fireplace, I'm usually wrapped up in the shawl.

SIZE

One size fits all

FINISHED MEASUREMENTS

Approximately 18"/45.5 cm wide × 72"/183 cm long

YARN

A: 2 skeins Suss Bomull (100% cotton; 4 ounces/114 grams; 190 yards/175 meters), color ecru

B: 3 skeins Suss Fuzzy (60% cotton/40% polyamide; 2 ounces/ 57 grams; 67 yards/62 meters), color henna

C: 2 skeins Suss Lash (60% cotton/40% polyester; 2 ounces/ 57 grams; 68 yards/63 meters), color cream

D: 3 skeins Suss Rainbow (40% mohair/30% cotton/25% wool/ 5% nylon; 1.5 ounces/43 grams; 65 yards/60 meters), color earthtone

E: 1 skein Suss Sparkle (70% cotton/15% lurex/15% nylon; 4 ounces/114 grams; 146 yards/135 meters), color naturale/silver

NOTIONS

1 pair size 11 (8 mm) needles

Tapestry needle

1 size G (4 mm) crochet hook

GAUGE

12 stitches and 18 rows = 4"/10 cm in stockinette stitch

making the shawl

With yarn A, cast on 54 stitches loosely.

Work in stockinette stitch (knit right-side rows, purl wrong-side rows) for 24 rows.

Change to yarn B and work in stockinette stitch for 16 rows.

Change to yarn C and work in stockinette stitch for 22 rows.

Change to yarn D and work in stockinette stitch for 20 rows.

Change to yarn E and work in stockinette stitch for 8 rows.

Change to yarn A and work in stockinette stitch for 8 rows.

Change to yarn E and work in stockinette stitch for 4 rows.

Change to yarn B and work in stockinette stitch for 8 rows.

Change to yarn C and work in stockinette stitch for 8 rows.

Change to yarn B and work in stockinette stitch for 8 rows.

Change to yarn E and work in stockinette stitch for 4 rows.

Change to yarn A and work in stockinette stitch for 8 rows.

Change to yarn E and work in stockinette stitch for 10 rows.

Change to yarn D and work in stockinette stitch for 22 rows.

Change to yarn C and work in stockinette stitch for 20 rows.

Change to yarn B and work in stockinette stitch for 16 rows.

Change to yarn A and work in stockinette stitch for 24 rows.

Change to yarn E and work in stockinette stitch for 10 rows.

Change to yarn D and work in stockinette stitch for 22 rows.

Change to yarn C and work in stockinette stitch for 20 rows.

Change to yarn E and work in stockinette stitch for 4 rows.

Change to yarn B and work in stockinette stitch for 16 rows.

Change to yarn A and work in stockinette stitch for 24 rows.

You will have 326 rows. Bind off loosely.

finishing

Weave in all loose ends with the tapestry needle.

With one strand of yarn A, work a single crochet stitch around the edge of the entire piece.

fringe

Cut 32 lengths of yarn B and 32 lengths of yarn C approximately 20"/51 cm each. Take one length of yarn B and one of yarn C and fold them in half. Insert the crochet hook into one of the corners of the shawl. Fold the 20"/51 cm lengths in half to form a loop and pull that loop through the shawl with the crochet hook. Then pull the lengths of yarn through that loop and tighten to make your first fringe tassel. On each of the narrow edges of the shawl, make approximately 16 fringe tassels placed about 1¼"/3 cm apart.

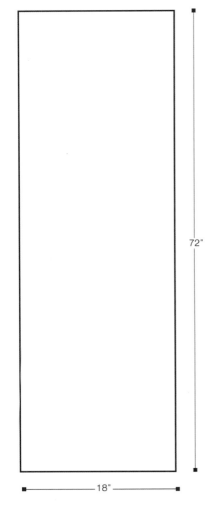

72"

18"

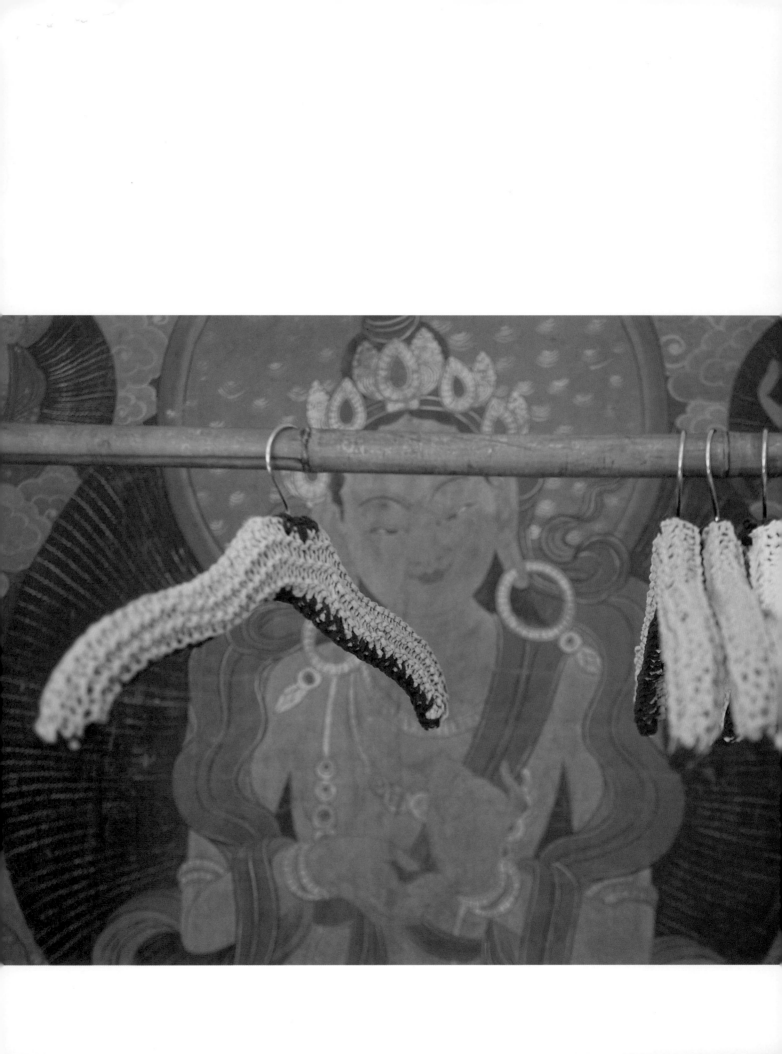

ultrasuede hanger cover

My grandmother crocheted or knitted hanger covers
like these. I hang my lingerie on them, and it never
slides off. They're actually better for all your clothes
than wire or plain wooden hangers.

ultrasuede hanger cover {easy}

Ultrasuede makes these hanger covers soft and inviting, and they're quite practical to make, too, in garter stitch. I have made them in so many colors—I have 200 hanging around my store to display our knitwear. Recently, as a wedding present, I made a set all in red for a guest closet.

SIZE
One size to fit standard dress hanger 18"/45.5 cm wide

FINISHED MEASUREMENTS
Approximately $16^{1}/_{2}$"/42 cm wide $\times$ $6^{1}/_{2}$"/16.5 cm long

Note: The width of the knitted piece is a bit smaller than the hanger so the piece will stay taut on the hanger.

YARN
A: 1 skein Suss Ultrasuede (100% ultrasuede; 4 ounces/114 grams; 70 yards/64 meters), color beige

B: 1 skein Suss Ultrasuede (100% ultrasuede; 4 ounces/114 grams; 70 yards/64 meters), color chocolate

OR

A: 1 skein Suss Ultrasuede (100% ultrasuede; 4 ounces/114 grams; 70 yards/64 meters), color cream

B: 1 skein Suss Ultrasuede (100% ultrasuede; 4 ounces/114 grams; 70 yards/64 meters), color red

NOTIONS
1 pair size $10^{1}/_{2}$ (6.5 mm) needles

Tapestry needle

1 wooden dress hanger approximately 18"/45.5 cm wide

1 size I (5.5 mm) crochet hook

GAUGE
12 stitches and 16 rows = 4"/10 cm

making the hanger cover

With yarn A, cast on 50 stitches loosely.

Work in garter stitch (knit every row) for 13 rows.

Make a hole for the metal hook:

Row 14: knit 24 stitches, bind off 2 stitches, and knit the remaining 24 stitches.

Row 15: knit 24 stitches, make 2 stitches, and knit the remaining 24 stitches.

Knit the next 13 rows for a total of 28 rows. Bind off loosely.

finishing

Weave in any loose ends with the tapestry needle.

With yarn B, work a single crochet around the buttonhole. Thread the wire hook of the hanger through the buttonhole and flatten the two sides of the cover against both sides of the hanger. You will need to stretch the cover slightly to make it fit snugly.

With this same color, join the two sides of the cover at the bottom of the hanger using single crochet. You may find it helpful to tie a couple waste knots to hold the two halves in place until they are crocheted together. Simply cut them off when you are done.

buttonhole for hook

6½"

16½"

kimono robe

Putting on this robe after your shower is like wrapping yourself in a luxurious cocoon. You'll feel like you're at a fancy resort without leaving home.

kimono robe {intermediate}

At my first trade show in Japan, I stayed at a hotel that provided a robe in a kimono cut. It's such an easy fit for either sex—and don't forget the kids! I decided to knit it in the softest cotton yarn I could find, which makes it warm and heavy. Your whole family will love the oversized pockets. This piece makes a great Father's Day or wedding present with an embroidered monogram.

SIZES

Adult: One size fits up to 50" chest

Kids: 2, (4, 6 years)

FINISHED MEASUREMENTS

Length: 48" (25", 27", 29")

Back: 25" (17", 18", 19")

YARN

Adult: 37 skeins Suss Natural (65% cotton/35% rayon; 2 ounces/ 57 grams; 76 yards/70 meters)

Children's sizes

2 years: 17 skeins Suss Natural (65% cotton/35% rayon; 2 ounces/57 grams; 76 yards/70 meters)

4 years: 18 skeins Suss Natural

6 years: 20 skeins Suss Natural

NOTIONS

1 pair size 13 (9 mm) knitting needles (24"/61 cm circular needles recommended)

1 pair size 7 (4.5 mm) knitting needles

6 stitch markers

Tapestry needle

1 size H (5 mm) crochet hook

Safety pins or sewing pins

Knitting row counter (recommended)

GAUGE

9 stitches and 12 rows = 4"/10 cm in stockinette stitch with size 13 needles and two strands of yarn

18 stitches and 12 rows = 4"/10 cm in one-by-one rib stitch with size 7 needles and two strands of yarn

making the adult robe

sleeves

Cast on 36 stitches with the larger needles and two strands of yarn. Work in stockinette stitch (knit right-side rows, purl wrong-side rows) for 9 rows. Starting with row 10, increase 1 stitch at the beginning and end of every sixth row (Rows 10, 16, 22, and so on), until piece measures 19"/48 cm.
Make two sleeves.

back

With the larger needles, cast on 56 stitches with two strands of yarn. Work in stockinette stitch for 36"/91.5 cm, approximately 108 rows, ending with a wrong-side row. Place markers on either side of this row to help guide you in attaching the armholes later (see diagram). You can use stitch markers or small pieces of contrasting yarn. Continue working in stockinette stitch for another 12"/30.5 cm, approximately 36 rows, ending with a wrong-side row.

Loosely bind off 21 stitches and place a marker. Bind off 14 more stitches and place a marker. These markers will guide you in attaching the neck piece later. Bind off the remaining 21 stitches.

right front

With the larger needles and two strands of yarn, cast on 41 stitches. Work in stockinette stitch for 106 rows. For the next 8 rows, continue in stockinette stitch, increasing one stitch at the end of every wrong-side row and the beginning of every right-side row (49 stitches total). Continue to work in stockinette stitch for another 32 rows (146 rows total).

To make the shoulder seam, bind off 21 stitches at the beginning of Row 147 and knit the remaining 28 stitches. Place a marker at the end of the row.

Work in stockinette stitch for another 11 rows. Begin shaping the collar by binding off 2 stitches at the beginning of Rows 159–162 (20 stitches total). Bind off loosely.

left front

With the larger needles and two strands of yarn, cast on 41 stitches. Work in stockinette stitch for 106 rows. For the next 8 rows, continue in stockinette stitch, increasing one stitch at the beginning of every wrong-side row and the end of every right-side row (49 stitches total). Continue to work in stockinette stitch for another 32 rows (146 rows total).

To make the shoulder seam, place a marker at the beginning of Row 147. Knit 28 stitches and bind off the remaining 21 stitches loosely. Tie off the end.

Rejoin the yarn to the last stitch of the previous row and work in stockinette stitch for another 11 rows. Begin shaping the collar by binding off 2 stitches at the beginning of Rows 159–162 (20 stitches total). Bind off loosely.

pockets

With the larger needles and two strands of yarn, cast on 16 stitches. Work in stockinette stitch until piece measures 11"/28 cm. Bind off loosely.

Make two pockets.

belt

With the smaller needles, cast on 11 stitches with two strands of yarn. Work in a one-by-one rib stitch for approximately 64"/163 cm.

finishing

Weave in any remaining loose ends with the tapestry needle.

Starting at the bottom of the right front piece, fold over the collar strip $2^1/2$"/6 cm, or about 5 stitches, towards the back and pin the edging and collar down. Hem the collar strip to the back of the right front piece using one strand of yarn (Note: use one strand for all joining and hemming). Leave the small openings at the top and bottom edges unclosed. Repeat the process for the left front piece.

Pin together back neck seam and close with invisible vertical join. With the right sides facing each other, pin the top edge of the back piece to the top edges of the right and left front pieces using the stitch markers on the back piece as your guides. The 21 stitches on either side of the stitch markers correspond to the 21 bind-off stitches on the front pieces. Sew the shoulder and neck seams.

Fold sleeves lengthwise with right sides facing each other. Pin and sew the sleeve seams with backstitch close to edge. Turn the cuffs over, wrong side facing out, approximately 2"/5 cm, and attach them to the outside of the sleeves with small tacking stitches. You can adjust the size of the cuffs to fit the length of your arms.

Pin the sleeves to the armhole sections of the back and front pieces. Use the stitch markers to guide you. Sew sleeves into armholes. Pin and sew up the side seams.

Fold over $1^1/2$"/4 cm from the top of one of the pocket pieces towards the front and pin it down. Sew this folded cuff to the front of the pocket. Repeat this process for the other pocket. Pin the pockets to the right and left front pieces 18"/46 cm from the bottom edge and 6"/15 cm (4"/10 cm) from the side collar edges.

With the crochet hook and two strands of yarn, work a single crochet stitch around the entire bottom hem of the robe.

To attach the belt, crochet a chain for each side of robe approximately 3"/8 cm long using two strands of yarn. Form the chains into loops and attach with the tapestry needle to the side seams of the robe about 29"/74 cm from the bottom hem. String the belt through these two loops.

making the child's robe

With the larger needles, cast on 32 (34, 34) stitches with two strands of yarn. Work in stockinette stitch (knit right-side rows, purl wrong-side rows) for 9 rows. Starting with Row 10, increase 1 (1, 1) stitch at the beginning and end of every ten rows until piece measures 13" (14", 15"). Bind off loosely.

Make two sleeves.

back

With the larger needles, cast on 38 (41, 43) stitches with two strands of yarn. Work in stockinette stitch for 19"/48 cm (20"/51 cm, 21"/53 cm), approximately 57 (60, 63) rows, ending with a wrong-side row. Place markers on either side of this row to help guide you in attaching the armholes later. Continue working in stockinette stitch for another 6"/15 cm (7"/18 cm, 8"/20.5 cm), approximately 18 (21, 24) rows, ending with a wrong-side row.

Loosely bind off 12 (13, 14) stitches and place a marker. Bind off 14 (15, 15) more stitches and place a marker. These markers will guide you in attaching the neck piece later. Bind off the remaining 12 (13, 14) stitches.

right front

With the larger needles and two strands of yarn, cast on 30 (31, 32) stitches. Work in stockinette stitch for 43 (47, 51) rows. For the next 6 (6, 6) rows, continue in stockinette stitch, increasing one stitch at the end of every wrong-side row and the beginning of every right-side row until you have a total of 36 (37, 38) stitches and 49 (53, 57) rows. Continue to work in stockinette stitch for another 28 (28, 30) rows—77 (81, 87) rows total.

To make the shoulder seam, on the next row, bind off 12 (13, 14) stitches and knit the remaining 24 (24, 24) stitches. Place a marker at the end of the row (see diagram).

Work in stockinette stitch for another 12 (12, 14) rows. Begin shaping the collar by binding off 2 stitches at the end of the next 4 (4,4) rows—94 (98, 106) rows and 16 (16, 16) stitches total. Bind off loosely.

left front

With the larger needles and two strands of yarn, cast on 30 (31, 32) stitches. Work in stockinette stitch for 43 (47, 51) rows. For the next 6 (6, 6) rows, increase 1 (1, 1) stitch at the beginning of every wrong-side row and the end of every right-side row until you have a total of 36 (37, 38) stitches and 49 (53, 57) rows. Continue to work in stockinette stitch for another 29 (29, 31) rows—78 (82, 88) rows total. Place a marker at end of this row. Knit 24 (24, 24) stitches and bind off the remaining 12 (13, 14) stitches loosely (see diagram). Tie off the end.

Rejoin the yarn to the last stitch of the previous row and begin shaping the collar by working in stockinette stitch for another 12 (12, 14) rows. Bind off 2 (2, 2) stitches at the beginning of the next 4 (4, 4) rows—16 (16,16) stitches and 94 (98, 106) rows total. Bind off loosely.

pockets

See the instructions for the adult version. The pocket is worked the same for all sizes.

belt

With smaller needles, cast on 7 stitches with two strands of yarn. Work in a one-by-one rib stitch for approximately 56"/142 cm. Weave in all loose ends with a tapestry needle.

finishing

Weave in any remaining loose ends with the tapestry needle.

Starting at the bottom of the right front piece, fold over the collar strip $2^1/4"$/6 cm, or about 5 stitches, towards the back and pin the edging and collar down (see diagram). Hem the collar strip to the back of the right front piece using one strand of yarn (Note: Use one strand for all joining and hemming). Leave the small openings at the top and bottom edges unclosed. Repeat the process with the left front piece.

Pin together back neck seam and close with invisible vertical join. With the right sides facing each other, pin the top edge of the back piece to the top edges of the right and left front pieces using the stitch markers on the back piece as your guides. The 12 (13, 14) stitches on either side of the stitch markers correspond to the 12 (13, 14) bind-off stitches on the front pieces. Sew the shoulder and neck seams.

Fold sleeves lengthwise right sides facing each other. Pin and sew the sleeve seams with backstitch close to edge. Turn the cuffs over, wrong side facing out, approximately $1^1/4"$/4 cm, and attach them to the outside of the sleeves. You can adjust the size of the cuffs to fit the length of your arms.

Pin the sleeves to the armhole sections of the back and front pieces. Use the stitch markers to guide you. Attach the sleeves. Pin and sew up the side seams.

Fold over $1^1/2"$/4 cm from the top of one of the pocket pieces towards the front and pin it down. Sew this folded cuff to the front of the pocket. Repeat this process for the other pocket. Pin the pockets to the right and left front pieces 8"/20 cm from the bottom edge and 4"/10 cm from the side collar edges.

With the crochet hook and two strands of yarn, work a single crochet stitch around the entire bottom hem of the robe.

To attach the belt, crochet a chain for each side of robe approximately 3"/8 cm long using two strands of yarn. Form the chain into a loop and attach with the tapestry needle to the side seams of the robe about 14"/ 35.5 cm up from the bottom hem.

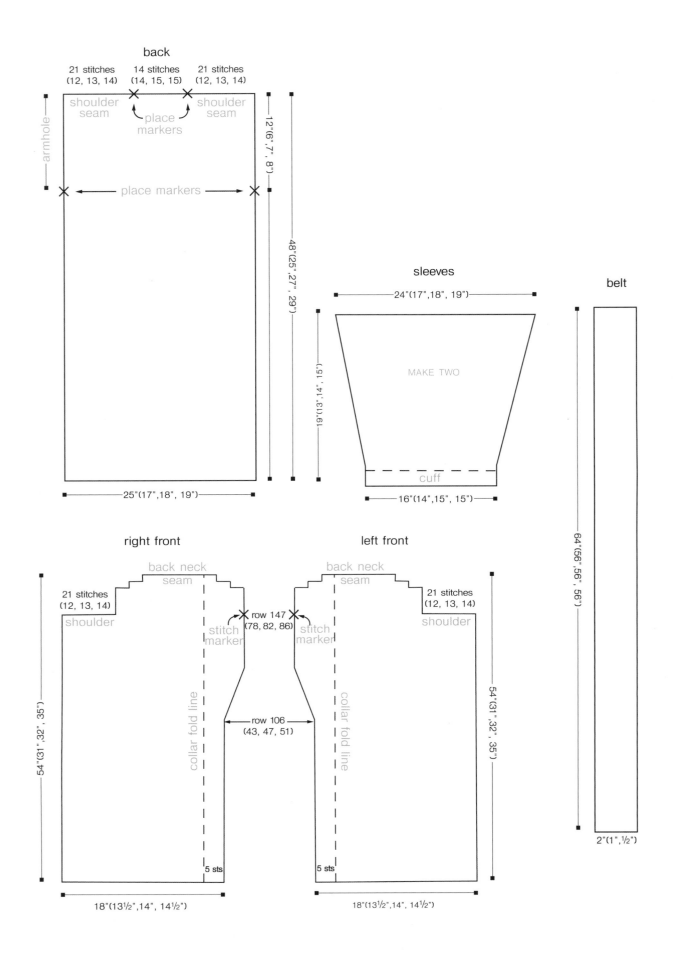

back

21 stitches (12, 13, 14) 14 stitches (14, 15, 15) 21 stitches (12, 13, 14)

shoulder seam ↰ place markers ↱ shoulder seam

armhole

12"(6", 7", 8")

← place markers →

48"(25", 27", 29")

25"(17",18", 19")

sleeves

← 24"(17",18", 19") →

MAKE TWO

19"(13", 14", 15")

cuff

16"(14",15", 15")

belt

64"(56",56", 56")

2"(1", ½")

right front

back neck seam

21 stitches (12, 13, 14)

shoulder

collar fold line

row 147 (78, 82, 86)

stitch marker

54"(31", 32", 35")

row 106 (43, 47, 51)

5 sts

18"(13½",14", 14½")

left front

back neck seam

21 stitches (12, 13, 14)

shoulder

collar fold line

stitch marker

54"(31", 32", 35")

5 sts

18"(13½",14", 14½")

luxurious bedcover

This is one bedspread you definitely will want to display in all its glory and not keep folded up at the bottom of your bed.

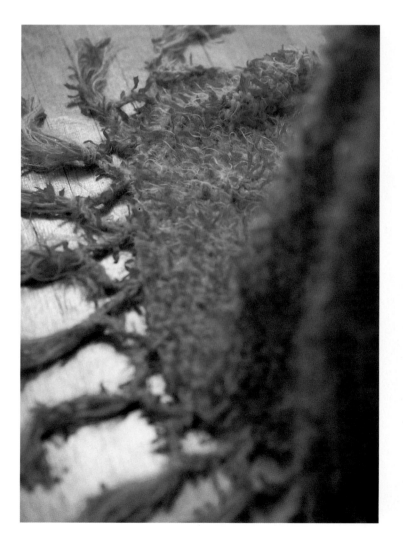

luxurious bedcover {easy}

When you lie down on this intensely colored bedspread, you'll feel as if you're being transported into an exotic fantasy. It's definitely an investment of both time and money, but you will have a gorgeous masterpiece, an heirloom, or an incredible gift at the end. The edges are crocheted and then fringe is attached, which gives it that fanciful touch.

FINISHED MEASUREMENTS

64"/162.5 cm wide × 80" long/203 cm (not including fringe)

Note: Comforter and mattress sizes vary a great deal. Take the time to get the measurements of your bed or of a bedspread you already like. When measuring your mattress, add at least 15"/38 cm to the length and 30"/76 cm to the width of your mattress to make a comfortably sized cover for your bed.

YARN

43 skeins Suss Butterfly (50% cotton/50% polyamide; 2 ounces/ 57 grams; 52 yards/48 meters), color orange

NOTIONS

1 pair size 13 (9 mm) circular needles, 47"/119 cm long

1 size H (5 mm) crochet hook

Large tapestry needle

GAUGE

11 stitches and 15 rows = 4"/10 cm in seed stitch

making the bedcover

Cast on 176 stitches loosely.

Work in seed stitch until piece measures 80"/203 cm, or approximately 300 rows.

Row 1: Knit 1, purl 1; repeat until the end of the row.

Row 2: Purl 1, knit 1; repeat until the end of the row.

Bind off loosely.

finishing

Weave in ends with the tapestry needle.

With the crochet hook and one strand of the yarn, work a single crochet up both of the long sides of the bedspread. Tie off the yarn and weave in the loose ends.

Beginning on one corner of the bedspread, attach one end of the yarn with a small knot and weave in the tail so it doesn't show. Crochet a chain 15 stitches long and attach it using a single crochet stitch approximately 10 rows, or 2.5"/6.5 cm up one of the long sides of the bedspread where you have just completed the single crochet edging. Continue by making another chain 15 stitches long and attach it approximately 2.5"/6.5 cm farther up the side of the bedspread.

Repeat these chain stitch loops all the way up both sides of the blanket. You will have approximately 30 15-stitch chain loops that will hang loosely from the blanket in a sort of "V" shape. It is not important that you get the exact number of loops on both sides.

making the fringe

Cut approximately 180 lengths of yarn 11"/28 cm long. You will need three times as many lengths of yarn as the total number of "V" loops on the sides of your bedspread. So if you have 20 loops on either side (for a total of 40), you will need to cut 120 lengths of yarn. Start at one corner of the blanket and find the middle of the first chain loop (about 8 chain stitches—don't worry, you can just eyeball it). Take three of the lengths of yarn and fold them in half. Insert the crochet hook into the middle stitch of the first "V" and pull the lengths of yarn through with the loop formed by folding them in half. Then pull the six strands through that loop and tighten to make fringe. Repeat the same process for each "V" loop on both sides.

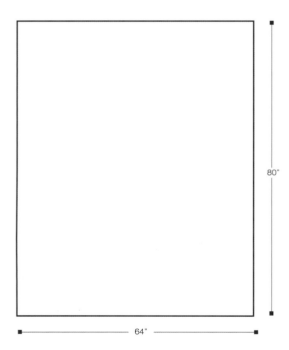

80"

64"

monogrammed guest towels

A touch of gold is what makes these guest
towels so memorable.

monogrammed guest towels

{easy}

I love anything sparkly—doesn't every girl? So I added gold fringe and embroidery to my guest towels, which are quite elegant in cream. The gold makes them even more luxurious, like bling for the bathroom. Silver would be equally jewel-like.

FINISHED MEASUREMENTS (WITHOUT FRINGE)

16"/41 cm × 26"/66 cm

YARN

A: 4 skeins Suss Snuggle (60% cotton/40% acrylic; 2 ounces/
57 grams; 126 yards/116 meters), color naturale

B: 2 balls Suss Lurex (65% metallic/35% lurex; 1 ounce/29 grams;
225 yards/208 meters), color gold

NOTIONS

1 pair size 8 (5 mm) needles

1 size G (4 mm) crochet hook

Tapestry needle

Straight pins

Tracing paper (optional)

GAUGE

18 stitches and 24 rows = 4"/10 cm in stockinette stitch

making the towel

Cast on 72 stitches with yarn A.

Work in stockinette stitch (knit right-side rows, purl wrong-side rows) until piece measures 26"/66 cm, or 156 rows, ending with a wrong-side row.

Bind off loosely.

Make two towels.

finishing

Weave in all loose ends with tapestry needle.

To embroider the monogram, photocopy the letter you want to make and enlarge it to about 3 1/2"/9 cm. You can also use tracing paper to trace the letter. Pin the photocopy or the tracing paper on to the towel with the letter centered 2"/5 cm from the bottom of the towel. With two strands of yarn B together, embroider the letter through the paper and the towel using chain stitches about 1/4"/1 cm each. When you're finished embroidering the letter, simply tear the paper away. You can use tweezers to pull away any stubborn little bits of paper that are left.

With one strand of yarn A and two strands of yarn B, use crochet hook to make a slip stitch and pull it through one of the towel's corners. Chain 1.

Crochet the following pattern around the edges of the towel: work a long single crochet 2 knit stitches from the edge, chain 1; work a long single crochet 4 knit stitches from the edge (be careful not to pull these long single crochets too tightly), chain 1; repeat around all four edges.

Repeat this pattern around all edges of the towel.

To make the fringe, cut 72 pieces of yarn A each 15"/38 cm long. Using 4 lengths held together attach fringe with the crochet hook by folding each group in half and pulling folded loop through the edge of the towel. Pull the ends through this loop and tighten. Attach 9 fringe tassels at each of the narrow edges of the towel, spacing them about 1 3/4"/4 cm apart.

Repeat the embroidery, edging, and fringe on the second towel.

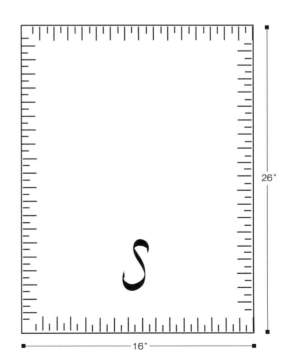

eyeglass case with button closure

I always have a hard time finding my eyeglasses in my purse. This fun case makes it so easy to find your glasses!

eyeglass case
with button closure {easy}

With its two-button string closure, this case makes a colorful accessory, whether
you keep it in your purse or in your bedroom, and the yarn doesn't scratch lenses.
Cell phones fit in it as well. Instead of the variegated pinks, you could make it in
brown for a man.

SIZE OF FINISHED CASE

$6^{1}/_{2}$"/16.5 cm × $3^{3}/_{4}$" /9.5 cm when closed

FINISHED MEASUREMENTS

$3^{1}/_{2}$"/9 cm X $14^{1}/_{2}$" /37 cm

YARN

A: 1 skein Suss Coolaid (85% acrylic/15% wool; 2 ounces/
57 grams; 90 yards/83 meters), color burgundy

B: 1 skein Suss Ultrasuede (100% ultrasuede; 4 ounces/114 grams;
70 yards/64 meters), color rose

NOTIONS

1 pair size 9 (5.5 mm) knitting needles

1 size G (4 mm) crochet hook

2 abalone shell buttons, 1"/2.5 cm in diameter

Large tapestry needle

Sewing needle and thread in a complementary color

GAUGE

14 stitches and 19 rows = 4"/10 cm in stockinette stitch

making the eyeglass case

Since you will be working with two strands of yarn A throughout,
start by making two balls from the single skein.

Drawing from both balls, cast on 12 stitches.

Knit in stockinette stitch (knit right-side rows, purl wrong-side rows),
until piece measures $14^{1}/_{2}$"/37 cm or 68 rows.

Bind off stitches loosely.

finishing

Weave in all loose ends with the tapestry needle.

With a double strand of yarn A, work a single crochet across the cast-on edge of your knitted rectangle. This will be the edge of the eyeglass opening. Measure 3"/8 cm from the cast-off edge and fold the crocheted cast-off edge, wrong sides together, to that point (about 5½"/14 cm from the bottom fold). Join the front and back together with single crochet stitch. Start at the bottom of the eyeglass case (at the fold) and work your way around all the outside edges of the case, including the flap (see photograph).

Using sewing needle and thread attach a button 1"/2.5 cm down from top edge centered across the width. Attach second button 2¼"/5.5 cm down from inside top edge centered across the width.

Whipstitch around the entire case with yarn B. Tie a 12"/30.5 cm piece of yarn B to the top button shank, and an 8"/20.5 cm piece of yarn B to the bottom button shank. Loop this decorative closure around the buttons twice to secure.

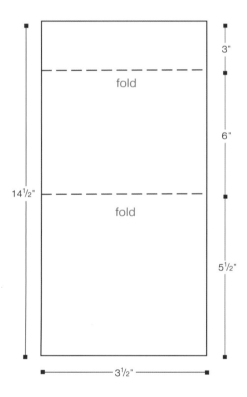

drawstring shoe bag

Color coordinate this cotton drawstring bag with your shoes so you can find them easily in a suitcase or closet.

drawstring shoe bag {easy}

My passion isn't handbags or jewelry: it's shoes. And I mean good shoes. I think I have about fifty pairs. Because I travel a lot, a shoe bag is essential. A hand-knit shoe bag is much nicer than a plastic bag, and you don't get buckles poking through.

I have many shoe bags, but this one, in natural cotton with leather and beads, is for my most expensive and beautiful pairs of shoes. They rest well when I travel. The handmade shoes in the photo are by Calleen Cordero, one of my favorite shoe designers.

FINISHED MEASUREMENTS

16"/41 cm × 34"/86.5 cm

YARN

A: 5 skeins Suss Twisted (100% cotton; 2.5 ounces/71 grams; 108 yards/98 meters), color natural

B: 1 skein Suss Ultrasuede (100% ultrasuede; 4 ounces/114 grams; 70 yards/64 meters), color chocolate

NOTIONS

1 pair size 8 (5 mm) needles

Tapestry needle

1 size G (4 mm) crochet hook

16 wooden beads, 1"/2.5cm diameter or large enough to thread Ultrasuede through

Straight pins

GAUGE

18 stitches and 22 rows = 4"/10 cm in stockinette stitch

making the shoe bag

Cast on 72 stitches with the size 8 needles in yarn A and work in stockinette stitch (knit right-side rows, purl wrong-side rows) until piece measures 34"/86.5 cm or approximately 187 rows.

Bind off loosely.

To knit the drawstring casing, cast on 144 stitches with yarn A.

Work in stockinette stitch for 11/20/4 cm.

Bind off loosely.

finishing

Weave in all loose ends with tapestry needle.

Fold the bag in half, right sides together, and sew sides together securely. When you are finished seaming, turn the bag right-side out. Finish the top edge of bag by working one row of single crochet all the way around.

Pin the drawstring casing to the bag 2"/5 cm below the top edge. Begin and end at a side seam, leaving an opening for the drawstring at both ends. Whipstitch the casing to the bag.

To make drawstrings, cut yarn B into 4 pieces each 50"/127 cm long. Thread strings through casing one at a time with tapestry needle. Tie two beads securely onto each end of the drawstrings. Make decorative knots in the drawstrings as desired.

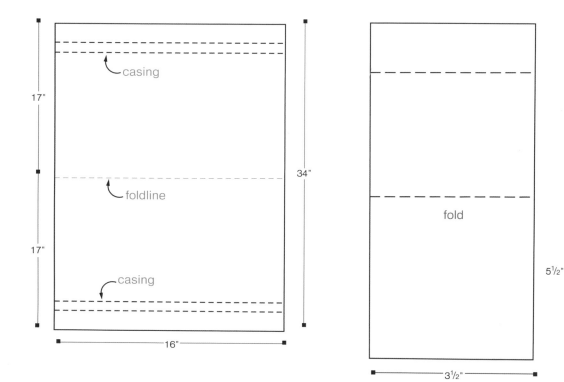

yarn substitution guide

The following guide, organized by yarn weight (as defined by the Craft Yarn Council of America), lists all the Suss yarns called for in this book and offers suggestions for substitution based on yarn's fiber content. As always, if you're not sure whether a particular yarn can be used as a substitute, try knitting a swatch first—does the gauge match? The fabric should also be similar in drape, texture, and appearance. Lastly, since the amount of yarn per skein varies, be sure to base substitution on the total yardage called for rather than the number of skeins.

(3) = DK, Light Worsted Yarn   (5) = Chunky, Craft, Rug

(4) = Worsted, Afghan, Aran yarn   (6) = Bulky, Roving

(3) LIGHT

Suss Angora: Any angora or cashmere blend yarn of comparable weight

Suss Lurex: Any lightweight lurex blend yarn

Suss Mohair: Any comparable mohair yarn

Suss Perle Cotton: Any lightweight fine cotton yarn

Suss Perle Variegated: Any variegated, lightweight, fine cotton yarn

Suss Ultrasoft: Any novelty viscose alpaca-nylon-blend yarn of comparable weight

Suss Ull: Any lightweight, fine merino wool yarn

(4) MEDIUM

Suss Alpaca: Any medium-weight alpaca-blend yarn of comparable weight

Suss Bomull: Any 100% cotton yarn of comparable weight

Suss Cotton: Any matte cotton yarn of comparable weight

Suss Feather: Any polyamide fuzzy yarn of medium weight

Suss Spacedye: Any variegated, medium-weight, cotton or wool yarn

(**4**) MEDIUM CONTINUED

Suss Speckled: Any medium-weight speckled-cotton yarn

Suss Snuggle: Any soft cotton or cotton-wool blend of comparable weight

Suss Twisted: Any medium-weight slub cotton

(**5**) BULKY

Suss Brushed Alpaca: Any bulky alpaca yarn of comparable weight

Suss Bunny: Any bulky polyamide yarn

Suss Butterfly: Any novelty cotton-polyamide blend yarn

Suss Candy: Any bulky mohair-rayon-polyester novelty blend yarn with lash effect

Suss Coolaid: Any bulky wool yarn with slub texture

Suss Fuzzy: Any textured cotton-nylon blend yarn

Suss Lash: Any matted cotton yarn mixed with long lash polyester

Suss Lux: Any bulky, soft, cotton blend yarn with fuzzy microfiber

Suss Natural: Any soft, chunky cotton-rayon hand blend

Suss Rainbow: Any comparable mohair yarn mixed with a fine cotton variegated yarn

Suss Sparkle: Any matte cotton yarn mixed with lurex of comparable weight

Suss Ultrasuede: Any bulky flat yarn or ribbon tape

(**6**) SUPER BULKY

Suss Fantasy: Any novelty blend yarn of comparable weight

Suss Handpainted: Any super bulky wool yarn of comparable weight

index of projects and yarns

This guide, illustrated by Suss, is organized by chapter so you can quickly determine which yarns you'll need to knit up your favorite projects.

living room

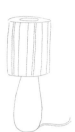

LIVELY STRIPED LAMPSHADE, PAGE 14

Suss Cotton [100% cotton]

(**4**) MEDIUM

LEAF LAMPSHADE, PAGE 18

Suss Mohair [76.5% mohair/17.5 wool/6% nylon]

(**3**) LIGHT

Suss Cotton [100% cotton]

(**4**) MEDIUM

BUTTONED-UP CURTAIN TIEBACK, PAGE 24

Cotton twill tape

(**4**) MEDIUM

BIG PILLOW COVER, PAGE 28

Suss Coolaid [85% acrylic/15% wool]
Suss Candy [40% mohair/30% rayon/30% polyester]
Suss Fuzzy [60% cotton/40% nylon]

(**5**) BULKY

Suss Feather [100% polyamide]

(**4**) MEDIUM

BASKETWEAVE PILLOW, **PAGE 32**

Suss Cotton [100% cotton]

4 MEDIUM

JUTE COASTERS, **PAGE 36**

Natural jute twine

4 MEDIUM

KNITTED ART, **PAGE 38**

Suss Twisted [100% cotton]

4 MEDIUM

Suss Mohair [76.5% mohair/17.5 wool/6% nylon]

3 LIGHT

OTTOMAN COZY, **PAGE 42**

Suss Handpainted [100% wool]

6 SUPER BULKY

ART WALL HANGING, **PAGE 46**

Suss Speckled   [90% wool/10% cotton]

4 MEDIUM

PASTEL PATCHWORK THROW, **PAGE 50**

Suss Lux [40% cotton/40% polyamide/20% rayon]
Suss Natural [65% cotton/35% rayon]

5 BULKY

dining room and kitchen

STRIPED SEAT COVERS, **PAGE 58**

Suss Bomull [100% cotton]

(**4**) MEDIUM

Suss Bunny [100% polyamide]

(**5**) BULKY

BEADED PLACEMATS, **PAGE 62**

Suss Cotton [100% cotton]

(**4**) MEDIUM

CHAIR COVERS WITH RIBBON TIES, **PAGE 66**

Suss Brushed Alpaca [100% alpaca]

(**5**) BULKY

NAPKIN HOLDER WITH BUTTON, **PAGE 70**

Suss Ultrasuede [100% Ultrasuede]

(**5**) BULKY

CRYSTAL TABLE RUNNER, **PAGE 74**

Suss Angora [70% angora/30% nylon]
Suss Lurex [65% rayon/35% metallic]

(**4**) MEDIUM

KNITTED GUESTBOOK, **PAGE 78**

Suss Ultrasuede [100% Ultrasuede]

(**5**) BULKY

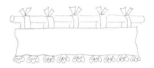

TWO-TONE KITCHEN CURTAINS, **PAGE 82**

Suss Twisted [100% cotton]

(**4**) MEDIUM

TOTE BAG, **PAGE 86**

Suss Perle Variegated [100% cotton]

(**3**) LIGHT

Suss Natural [65% cotton/35% rayon]
Suss Ultrasuede [100% Ultrasuede]

(**5**) BULKY

BASKETWEAVE RUG, PAGE 90

Suss Coolaid [85% acrylic/15% wool]

(**5**) BULKY

Suss Spacedye   [100% cotton]

(**4**) MEDIUM

EMBROIDERED VASE COVER, **PAGE 94**

Suss Ull [100% wool]
Suss Perle Cotton [100% cotton]

(**3**) LIGHT

bedroom and bath

ALPACA LAMPSHADES, **PAGE 102**

Suss Alpaca [100% alpaca]

(**4**) MEDIUM

SWEDISH BED CANOPY, **PAGE 106**

Suss Ultrasoft [40% viscose/30% alpaca/20% acrylic/10% nylon]

(**3**) LIGHT

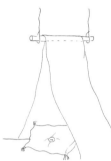

FANTASY PILLOWS, **PAGE 110**

Suss Fantasy [50% cotton/15% mohair/10% viscose/10% nylon, 10% polyester/5% wool]

(**6**) SUPER BULKY

MULTI-YARN SHAWL, **PAGE 112**

Suss Bomull [100% cotton]

(**4**) MEDIUM

Suss Fuzzy [60% cotton, 40% nylon]
Suss Lash [60% cotton/40% polyester]
Suss Rainbow [40% mohair/30% cotton/25% wool/ 5% nylon]
Suss Sparkle [70% cotton/15% lurex/15% nylon]

(**5**) BULKY

ULTRASUEDE HANGER COVER, **PAGE 118**

Suss Ultrasuede [100% Ultrasuede]

(**5**) BULKY

KIMONO ROBE, PAGE 122

Suss Natural [65% cotton/35% rayon]

(5) BULKY

LUXURIOUS BEDCOVER, PAGE 130

Suss Butterfly [50% cotton/50% polyamide]

(5) BULKY

MONOGRAMMED GUEST TOWELS, PAGE 134

Suss Snuggle [60% cotton/40% acrylic]

(4) MEDIUM

Suss Lurex [65% nylon/35% metallic]

(3) LIGHT

EYEGLASS CASE WITH BUTTON CLOSURE, PAGE 138

Suss Coolaid [85% acrylic/ 15% wool]
Suss Ultrasuede [100% Ultrasuede]

(5) BULKY

DRAWSTRING SHOE BAG, PAGE 142

Suss Twisted [100% slubcotton]

(4) MEDIUM

Suss Ultrasuede [100% Ultrasuede]

(5) BULKY

resources

yarn

Suss yarn is available at the Suss Design store located at 7350 Beverly Boulevard, Los Angeles, California 90036 (telephone: 323-954-9637). The store stocks a complete line of yarns from all the best manufacturers and Suss brand yarns. Shoppers can also find needles, patterns, and a complete collection of notions (buttons, beads, crochet, and leather decorations) needed for projects in Suss's books. Specialty items include Suss's hand cream for knitters and a customized blend of tea.

Knitters around the country can purchase Suss yarns, as well as many of the notions featured in this book, at the Suss Design website, www.sussdesign.com. Here's a list of stores that carry Suss Yarn:

ALASKA
**Yarn Branch of
The Quilt Tree**
341 E. Benson #5
Anchorage, AK 99503
907-561-4115

CALIFORNIA
Article Pract
5010 Telegraph Ave.
Oakland, CA 94609
510-595-7875

Three Dog Knit
475 N. Lake Blvd.
Suite 103
Tahoe City, CA 96145
530-583-0001

CONNECTICUT
Knitting Central
582 Post Rd. East
Westport, CT 06880
203-454-4300

DISTRICT OF COLUMBIA
Stitch DC
5520 Connecticut Ave., NW
Washington, DC 20015
202-237-8306

ILLINOIS
Chix with Stix
7316 W. Madison St.
Forest Park, IL 60130
708-366-6300

Loopy Yarns
719 South State St.
Chicago, IL 60605
312-583-9276

MINNESOTA
Digs
310 Division St. South
Northfield, MN 55057
507-664-9140

NEW YORK
Wild Wools
732 South Ave.
Rochester, NY 14620
585-271-0960

OKLAHOMA
Loops
2042 Utica Sq. West
Tulsa, OK 74114
918-742-9276

PENNSYLVANIA
Loop
1914 South St.
Philadelphia, PA 19146
215-893-9939

CANADA
Room 6
4389 Gallant Ave.
North Vancouver, BC
Canada V7G1L1

FOR INFORMATION ON SUBSTITUTING ANY OF THE YARNS USED IN THIS BOOK, PLEASE SEE THE YARN SUBSTITUTION GUIDE ON PAGE 146.

other materials and notions

Home Knits is as much about home design as it is about knitting. As such, some of the projects call for materials and notions more readily available at the hardware store than at your local yarn shop. The list below will help you find any non-knitting items you might need to complete the projects. You can go to the company's website to locate the store nearest you. If the resource is only online, that is indicated as well.

FABRIC AND CRAFT SUPPLIES

For these items:

Snap fasteners and fabric (Project: Tote Bag)
Leather and leather punch (Project: Basketweave Pillow)
Organza ribbon (Project: Chair Covers with Ribbon Ties)

Go here:

A. C. Moore	Jo-Ann Fabric & Crafts	Tandy
888-686-8965	818-739-4120	800-433-3201
www.acmoore.com	www.joann.com	www.tandyleather.com
CraftA.com (online)	Michael's	Waverly Fabrics
888-327-2382	800-642-4235	800-423-5881
www.crafta.com	www.michaels.com	www.waverly.com

HARDWARE/HOME IMPROVEMENT/GARDEN SUPPLY

For these items:

Bamboo rods (Projects: Art Wall Hanging, Swedish Bed Canopy)
Staple gun (Projects: Striped Seat Covers, Knitted Art)
Small hooks (Project: Knitted Art)
Ceiling hooks (Project: Swedish Bed Canopy)

Go here:

Home Depot	Lowe's
www.homedepot.com	www.lowes.com

FURNITURE/HOME FURNISHINGS

For these items:

      Drum lampshades (8", 13", and 20") and lamps (Projects: Lively Striped
      Lampshade, Leaf Lampshade, Alpaca Lampshade)
      Floor pillow (24" x 24") and bolster pillow (Projects: Big Pillow Cover,
      Basketweave Pillow, Fantasy Pillow)
      Ottoman (Project: Ottoman Cozy)
      Seat cushions (14") and chairs (Projects: Striped Seat Cushions, Chair Covers
      with Ribbon Ties)
      Vases (5") (Project: Embroidered Vase Cover)
      Hangers (Project: Ultrasuede Hanger Cover)

Go here:

Bed, Bath & Beyond	Pier 1 Imports
800-462-3966	800-245-4595
www.bedbathandbeyond.com	www.pier1.com
Ikea	Target
800-434-4532	www.target.com
www.ikea.com/ms/enUS/	

CRYSTAL, BEADS, AND BUTTONS

For these items:

      Wooden buttons, horn buttons, abalone buttons (Projects: Big Pillow Cover
      Buttoned-Up Curtain Tieback, Napkin Holder with Button, Tote Bag, Knitted
      Guestbook, Eyeglass Case)
      Beaded trim (Project: Beaded Placements)
      Austrian beads (Project: Crystal Table Runner)

Go here:

As Cute As a Button	Beadworks
619-223-2555	800-232-3761
www.ascuteasabutton.com	www.beadworks.com/us/
Auntie's Beads	JewelrySupply (online)
866-262-3237	866-380-7464
www.auntiesbeads.com/Home.aspx	www.jewelrysupply.com

ART SUPPLIES

For these items:

    Canvas (Project: Knitted Art)
    Notepaper (Project: Knitted Guestbook)

Go here:

Flax	Kate's Paperie	Pearl Paints
888-352-9278	800-809-9880	800-451-7327
www.flaxart.com	www.katespaperie.com	www.pearlpaint.com

about the author

Suss Cousins, the author of two previous knitting books, grew up in Sweden, where her grandmother taught her to knit and where, at the age of nineteen, she opened her first boutique. After moving to New York in 1982, she tended bar by night and knit sweaters by day.

Since coming to the United States, she has grown her business from designing custom pieces for a small roster of loyal clients to designing complete lines of fashion knitwear for men, women, and children. Her inspired designs are available at her retail store in Los Angeles as well as at boutiques and department stores throughout the country, including Bergdorf Goodman, Barney's, and Neiman Marcus.

Suss also designs for television and film. Suss's unique knit costumes have been featured in movies such as *Last Holiday, Underdog, Cat in the Hat, Shall We Dance, The Matrix, Master and Commander, Men in Black,* and *How the Grinch Stole Christmas,* and on TV shows such as *The OC, Gilmore Girls, Curb Your Enthusiasm, Will and Grace,* and *Friends.*

Knitters clamor for her yarns and patterns and flock to her website (www.sussdesign.com) and her popular classes. Suss's own yarn brand, along with a special knitter's hand cream and a soothing tea, is now available in yarn shops nationwide. In addition, Suss has produced an instructional DVD on knitting.

Suss lives in Los Angeles with her husband and two daughters.

Acknowledgments

It has been an exciting experience to work on this book and to come up with ideas to make your home special and cozy and handcrafted but with a modern twist. Thanks to all my friends, who are always so supportive and enthusiastic, as well as to my knitting students, who energize me to create even more. My message to you is be positive, and don't be afraid to take my ideas into your home. It's easier and more satisfying than you think!

Special thanks to:

Yoshie Shirai Eenigenburg, who once again helped me put a book together, especially with styling the photographs to reflect my vision. You are an incredible person.

Michael Weschler, a photographer who truly has a talent for making a still come alive. It was a pleasure working with you.

Kate Lonsdale, who helped me with all the patterns. I can't wait to work with you again!

Robin Dellabough and Lark Productions for continuing to bring my knitting to the public and to make my message clear.

Karen Greenwald for outstanding technical editing.

Everyone at Suss Design Inc. Thanks for your hard work and for standing by me during thick and thin. I love you all.

Shawna Mullen, Rosy Ngo, Lauren Monchik, Elizabeth Wright, Christina Schoen, and Amy Sly at Potter Craft. It's great to work with such a creative and fun team.

Evolutionary Media and Jennifer Gross. We have been through many things together, so thanks for always being supportive.

Robin Glaser for always saying yes to working with me on makeup and hair. You are a really good friend.

Elizabeth Lovins for your generous participation and for bringing the perfect dog, Roofis Petunia Parks.

Joanie Berkley for your beautiful flower arrangements.

Gisela Marin and Steven Werndorf, my favorite friends.

Jay Roberts—you are family.

Susan Balcunas, a friend with great style.

Vicki Andersson and her orange cat, Bongo.

Lesley Anton for her incredible lamp bases.

Calleen Cordero for her signature shoes.

My brother Peter—you're finally part of my book.

My two gorgeous girls, Hanna and Viveka. To see you grow and to have you in my life makes everything worth living for.

And to Brian, a rock that I can lean on. Every day that I get to spend with you in the sunshine makes me believe that what I do is for a great reason. I love you—thanks!

index

Art, knitted, 38–41
Art Wall Hanging, 46–49

Bed Canopy, Swedish, 106–9
Bedcover, Luxurious, 130–33
Bedroom and Bath, 98–145
Beginners
    Buttoned-Up Curtain Tieback,
        24–27
    Jute Coasters, 36–37

Chair Covers with Ribbon Ties, 66–69
Coasters, Jute, 36–37
Curtains
    Buttoned-Up Tieback for, 24–27
    Two-Tone Kitchen, 82–85

Decreasing stitches
    on a knit row, 48
    on a purl row, 48
Dining Room and Kitchen, 54–97

Easy
    Basketweave Rug, 90–93
    Big Pillow Cover, 28–31
    Crystal Table Runner, 74–77
    Drawstring Shoe Bag, 142–45
    Eyeglass Case with Button Closure,
        138–41
    Knitted Guestbook, 78–81
    Luxurious Bedcover, 130–33
    Monogrammed Guest Towels,
        134–37
    Napkin Holder with Button, 70–73
    Pastel Patchwork Throw, 50–53
    Ultrasuede Hanger Cover, 118–21
Experienced
    Art Wall Hanging, 46–49
    Chair Covers with Ribbon Ties,
        66–69
    Knitted Art, 38–41
Eyeglass Case with Button Closure,
    138–41

Guest towels, monogrammed, 134–37
Guestbook, knitted, 78–81

Hanger Cover, Ultrasuede, 118–21

Increasing stitches
    on a knit row, 48
    on a purl row, 48
Intermediate
    Alpaca Lampshade, 102–5
    Basketweave Pillow, 32–35
    Beaded Placemats, 62–65
    Embroidered Vase Cover, 94–97
    Fantasy Pillows, 110–13
    Kimono Robe, 122–29
    Leaf Lampshade, 18–23
    Lively Striped Lampshade, 14–17
    Multi-Yarn Shawl, 114–17
    Ottoman Cozy, 42–45
    Striped Seat Covers, 58–61
    Swedish Bed Canopy, 106–9
    Tote Bag, 86–89
    Two-Tone Kitchen Curtains, 82–85
Invisible join, 17
    Vertical, 22

Kimono Robe, 122–29
Lampshades
    Alpaca, 102–5
    Leaf, 18–23
    Lively Striped, 14–17
Living Room, 10–53

Napkin Holder with Button, 70–73

Ottoman Cozy, 42–45

Pillows
    Basketweave, 32–35
    Big Cover for, 28–31
    Fantasy, 110–13
Placemats, beaded, 62–65

Robe, Kimono, 122–29
Rug, Basketweave, 90–93

Seat Covers, Striped, 58–61
Shawl, Multi-Yarn, 114–17
Shoe Bag, Drawstring, 142–45
Swedish Bed Canopy, 106–9

Table Runner, Crystal, 74–77
Throw, Pastel Patchwork, 50–53
Tieback, Buttoned-Up Curtain, 24–27
Tote Bag, 86–89

Vase Cover, Embroidered, 94–97